THE GOOD GIRL'S GUIDE TO

Living in Sin

JOSELIN LINDER & ELENA DONOVAN MAUER

THE GOOD GIRL'S GUIDE TO

Living in Sin

THE NEW RULES FOR MOVING IN WITH YOUR MAN

Aadamsmedia

avon, massachusetts

Published by
Adams Media, an F+W Publications Company
57 Littlefield Street, Avon, MA 02322. U.S.A.
www.adamsmedia.com

ISBN 10: 1-59869-584-3
ISBN 13: 978-1-59869-584-7

Printed in the United States of America.

J I H G F E D C B A

Library of Congress Cataloging-in-Publication Data
is available from the publisher.

This publication is designed to provide accurate and authoritative information with regard to the subject matter covered. It is sold with the understanding that the publisher is not engaged in rendering legal, accounting, or other
professional advice. If legal advice or other expert assistance is required, the
services of a competent professional person should be sought.
—From a *Declaration of Principles* jointly adopted by a Committee of the
American Bar Association and a Committee of Publishers and Associations

Many of the designations used by manufacturers and sellers to distinguish
their product are claimed as trademarks. Where those designations appear
in this book and Adams Media was aware of a trademark claim, the designations have been printed with initial capital letters.

This book is available at quantity discounts for bulk purchases.
For information, please call 1-800-289-0963.

contents

acknowledgments

We would like to thank Molly Lyons and everyone at Delbourgo and Associates for such tremendous support and for making this book happen. Molly, we can't tell you enough how grateful we are for your faith, advice, encouragement, and friendship. Also to Adams Media, especially Jennifer Kushnier, for choosing us to write her idea, and Meredith O'Hayre, for making it lovely.

Joselin would also like to thank the Tigers at the Stoned Crow because it all began with them. To Aaron for moving in and proving that this advice is sound and for, well, moving in! Rhoda Linder and Hilary Griffith for being great early roommates. To William Linder and Jeromy for a courageous love of writing. And to Elena, what a pleasure! Thank you.

Elena, would of course like to thank Joselin for cracking her up and for always being able to look at things from a fresh perspective. Every time I couldn't fill in a blank, you did! To Tony, for never seeming to mind that I was writing all the time and for saying that this is the next book on his "to read" list. A good man is one who will be seen in public with a fuchsia-covered book just to support his wife. To my family, who gave me a love of books and writing and never told me there was anything I couldn't do—even live with my boyfriend.

Most of all, we'd like to thank the 100+ women who let us probe them about their personal lives and who gave us inspiration throughout the entire writing process. You shaped this book, and your advice and stories will be tasty food for thought for every woman that picks it up.

introduction:
cohabitation, past and present

The problem with not living together is that you really don't see a whole other side to the person. When I moved in with my boyfriend, I learned things that I didn't already know—even when I stayed over all the time. Cohabiting is completely different than just staying over. It really is like living with your best friend. I wouldn't have done it any differently. In today's world it just makes sense.

—Robin, teacher, Springfield, New Jersey

We don't know anyone under the age of fifty who calls it *living in sin* anymore—and not too many over fifty either. The whole *sin* part of it makes us think of something that would only be attempted by our shady fourth cousin who was once in juvie for robbing an ATM. But really, that's the way cohabitation was viewed just decades ago. Now it's so common that we have friends, coworkers, siblings, cousins, former roommates, and even parents who've lived with someone they care about without walking down the aisle first. Today, even the "good girl" cohabits with her boyfriend.

The numbers prove it. According to the Center for Disease Control and Prevention, 41 percent of American adult women under the age of forty-four have lived, unmarried, with a male partner.

There are a whopping 9.7 million Americans living with a romantic partner of the opposite sex. (This says nothing of the number of homosexual couples making it work.) The U.S. Census reports that ten times as many unmarried couples are sharing a home as were in 1960, and 72 percent more than in 1990.

A practice that was once considered taboo has now become as normal a way for people in a relationship to increase their commitment as getting pinned at the sock hop once was. Lucky us. We just love having a guy to curl up with on the couch when we get home.

Famous Unmarried Couples:
All the Cool Kids Are Living in Sin

Julie Taymor (director) and Elliot Goldenthal (composer)—He said, "We've spent 20 years being happily unmarried."

Angelina Jolie and Brad Pitt—a couple since 2005, have four kids, we think. We've lost count. 2006 quote from Brad: "Angie and I will consider tying the knot when everyone else in the country who wants to be married is legally able."

Larry Mullen Jr. (of U2) and Ann Acheson—they are high school sweethearts!

Oprah Winfrey and Stedman Graham—got engaged in 1992 but still have not married. Oprah's been quoted as saying, "I think the relationship as it is works really, really solidly well."

You Wouldn't Buy a Car Without Taking a Test Drive

So you're so crazy about this guy that you want to spend every free minute with him? Let's say you haven't decided to cohabit yet, but you spend every weekend together and on weeknights you often take turns toting DVDs and toothbrushes to each other's places. You might wonder what makes some women take that extra step to sharing major appliances, a lease, and a toilet with their boyfriends.

Well, it's usually that can't-get-enough-of-him feeling (often called love), mixed with at least one of the following scenarios:

The first, and perhaps most practical, is economics. Erika, a writer in New York City, cites money as the motivating factor for moving in with her guy: "It was the typical New York situation—housing! My roommates were moving out, and he and I spent almost every night together anyway. Financially, it made sense." Two people. One set of bills. An easy equation for saving some dough.

Social factors also play a role. Ambitious couples often don't have a lot of time to go out on a lot of dates, and cohabitation gives them the opportunity to fit "couple time" into their daily lives. Especially in areas of the country that are particularly sprawling or have large amounts of traffic, who wants to travel back and forth?

And why have a stranger for a roommate when you can share a home with someone you already care about?

More and more, couples are seeing cohabitation as the "next step" in their relationship, after dating. These couples already know they care about each other and want to get past the formality of dinner and movie dates.

"It was important to me to get to that level of intimacy with him," says Renee, a software sales tech in Columbus, Ohio. Living together is a way for couples to get closer emotionally—for many it is a way to achieve a new stage in the relationship. Something deeper. Something with a built-in snow-shoveler/cuddler combo.

One of the most popular reasons for cohabitation is to test those proverbial waters—decide whether you and this guy could make marriage work. "I think it's definitely a trial run for marriage," says Melissa, a writer in Brooklyn, New York. "Can you share a small sink and a toothbrush holder all the time? What do you expect from one another in terms of dividing up the work of having a home? It's important!"

But just as commonly, we found that many couples who decided to live together *knew* they wanted to get married but felt too young, too broke, or otherwise not quite ready to tie the knot. Maybe they were waiting until they finished their schooling, or they wanted to give their relationship a little more time before making the ultimate commitment, the way Carrie, an investment banker in New York City, and her guy did. "We both knew we were going to get married but we hadn't been dating long enough to actually take that step—only five months," says Carrie.

MOST COMMON REASONS TO LIVE WITH YOUR BOYFRIEND

Saving money. One lease is less expensive than two.

Lack of time. When you live together, you have more minutes to hang out together.

Liking each other. You're each other's best roommate candidates.

"The next step." Reaching a higher level of intimacy.

A trial run for marriage. Can you share your space and run a household together?

Knowing you want to marry. Just not quite yet.

Maybe Our Generation Needs Its Own Theme Song

There are many reasons to live together, but why has it only become so prevalent in recent decades? *USA Today* reports that today, most cohabiting couples are between the ages of twenty-four and thirty-four. So what makes our generation of young adults different from those in the past?

Judith, an administrative assistant in Pittsburgh, Pennsylvania, in her fifties, suggests it's a number of factors. "I think younger women have seen [my generation's] marriages fall apart, or seen us living in a marriage that is not so great, and you want to make smarter decisions. When I was single—the first time—good girls didn't leave home till they married; we didn't just go out and get an apartment. In fact, in college, there was a 10:30 P.M. curfew, and the college called your parents if you missed it," says Judith. "Why do I think you choose cohabitation? You don't want to make the mistakes we did."

She might be on to something here. We're not trying to say anyone did anything *wrong*, but our parents' generation is notorious for their divorce rate—unlike their parents before them, when they found themselves in an unhappy marriage, they were willing to call it quits. In many cases, if the relationship had major problems, that was a good thing—but divorce can be detrimental, especially where your children and your finances are concerned. Our generation, many of us having witnessed our parents' divorces, sees an opportunity to try to prevent divorce from the outset. By adding a few steps between going steady and wearing his ring, you give yourself more chances to know each other and to settle more fluidly into a life together.

"Being a child of divorced parents changes the way you look at marriage," says Jeanette, a special education teacher in Reston, Virginia. "I've always said that I would live with someone before I married them to make sure he was 'the one.'"

Also, women in our age group are more and more career-oriented. And we are more educated than ever before. "We are going to school longer, paying off loans longer, so having to work longer to get established, and then getting married later in life," says Hope, a corporate recruiter in Southampton, Pennsylvania.

Waiting longer to get married means we have time to live with guys we love beforehand. We don't have to find a husband before we can get the hell out of Mom and Dad's house. In fact, most of us already have experience supporting ourselves financially, so we don't feel we need a husband to "take care of us"—most of us just end up finding someone we love with whom we want to share a home. Marriage is not a necessity.

Of course, our generation, much to some of our grandparents' chagrin, has exhibited much more casual sexual behaviors. In fact, we're so open that we're not even trying to hide the fact that we're having premarital sex anymore. "Attitudes about sex have changed so much over the years," agrees Jody, a graphic designer in Falls Church, Virginia. "Birth control certainly changed things as well, giving both men and women more freedom to choose to have sex but not children."

are we doing better?

A 2007 report published by MSNBC says that the divorce rate is about 3.6 divorces per 1,000 people. That's the lowest it's been since 1970. The peak? 5.3 divorces per 1,000 people in 1981.

In many cases, it's just a matter of taking the time to make our own decisions about what we want for ourselves long-term. Call us selfish—or better yet, self-respecting—but many of us don't want to feel rushed, and we want to do everything we can do to end up fully considerate of our own best interests.

"Living together ultimately helped us decide on our future together. Knowing what direction I wanted to go in life was important for me," explains Lucy, a nurse in Bexley, Ohio.

Maybe it's also that we've become more and more accepting of lifestyles that are different from the traditional norm. Today, only one-third of American households are what was previously considered a "traditional family," defined as a married couple and their children. And therefore, we're more accepting of lifestyles that don't fit that mold to a tee. Proof? In one poll, 90 percent of people agreed that society "should value all types of families." Right on!

It should also be mentioned that the trailblazing of many gay and lesbian organizations have created a political voice for couples who are cohabitating. In fact, in many ways, these men and women, who are in most cases legally barred from the institution of marriage, have done a lot to raise questions about the importance of marriage itself. In this book, we do not in any way repute

WHY A RISE IN COHABITATION?

Trying to prevent divorce, something for which our parents' generation is notorious.

More education and drive for career success puts marriage later on the time line of life.

Independence. Now, we can move out of Mom and Dad's house without being married.

More open-minded attitudes about premarital sex.

Advances in birth control. Sex doesn't always mean babies anymore.

A more self-minded generation. We're taking the time to figure out what's best for us.

A greater acceptance of lifestyles that don't necessarily include being married with 2.5 kids.

the importance or merits of marriage. In fact, we think weddings are fun and think marriage on the whole is a great thing. Still, it is relevant to mention that due to many fundamental differences between hetero and homosexual couples that make cohabitation both easier and harder for each, this book has been written from a heterosexual perspective. Trust us, it's long enough as it is!

Still, many factors have contributed to opening the door to cohabitation as a respected and reasonable choice in a relationship. It is one that, once carefully considered, we think you can feel safe and even proud to make.

Scare Tactics: Fire, Brimstone, Divorce, and Poverty

You know the scare tactics we're talking about. Turn on the news and you learn how many germs live on the bottom of the average pocketbook and what's lingering on the sheets in the local hotels. (Uh, gross. We'd rather not know.) Then the anchors go on to warn you of local scam artists and identity thieves. Be afraid. Be *very* afraid.

People sometimes do the same with cohabitation, listing facts and figures from studies insinuating some kind of terrifying outcome from living together. (You'll have boils, we tell you! Boils and welts the size of golf balls!) And it can be scary. To be totally fair to you, we want to put those results out on the table, so here goes . . .

Some studies have found that couples living together before marriage are more likely to divorce. Others have said that unhappiness, poor health, poverty, and domestic violence are more common among unmarried couples than married ones. Still more:

accidental pregnancies are said to be significantly higher for couples that live together, as opposed to those who don't.

We honestly can't say "Screw 'em—don't believe a word!" Cohabitation is a serious decision that shouldn't be entered into without a second, third, or fourth thought. But think about it this way: Cohabitation practiced by such a large margin of the population is a fairly new phenomenon. The statistics about the longevity of the relationships aren't up-to-date. And they won't be for years.

Here's another explanation, quoted from the Alternatives to Marriage Project's Web site (*www.unmarried.org*):

> "These studies' conclusions are frequently misrepresented in the media. Basically, studies like these are comparing apples and oranges. Most couples today live together before they marry, and research shows that on average, the minority of couples who marry without living together tend to be more religious, more conservative, and more opposed to divorce, as one would expect. So these studies actually show that people who are more opposed to divorce are less likely to divorce—which is not particularly surprising. Researchers have found that when you 'control' for the differences between the two groups, the cohabitation-divorce link decreases considerably or vanishes entirely, depending on the study. The idea that living together ruins relationships is not supported in any research."

Also, some have refuted the stats about poverty and domestic violence because they include the living situation of people of all socioeconomic sectors.

"I think that often poor and already unhappy people fall into living together, because it's cheaper and easier, rather than a conscious, thought-out choice," weighs in Jen, a freelance writer in

Glen Ridge, New Jersey. "That skews the numbers, because when you drift into a major life decision, big problems are a natural fallout."

Further, statistics are just that. You should not be bound by them. Certainly acknowledge them, but don't stop there. The fact is, you wouldn't jump off a bridge just because everyone else was doing it. But what if no one was jumping off the bridge but the truth was that if you did, the water would feel fantastic? All we can do is take our own, unique situation and do what we feel is best for us. As long as you've thought the decision through and feel it's right, we think you're okay. You are not a statistic—and a negative statistic doesn't mean you're doomed.

Does waiting longer to get married reduce the risk of divorce? Check out these stats, as reported on *www.divorcerate.org*:

Age at marriage for those who divorce in America		
AGE	WOMEN	MEN
Under 20 years old	27.6%	11.7%
20 to 24 years old	36.6%	38.8%
25 to 29 years old	16.4%	22.3%
30 to 34 years old	8.5%	11.6%
35 to 39 years old	5.1%	6.5%

Your best comebacks when people bring up negative stats about living together include:

- We have thought through our decision and are not taking it lightly.

- Religion is not factored into the research. If you don't believe in cohabiting, you probably don't believe in divorce—and that's a minority of the population. More liberal couples tend to live together, just as more liberal people tend to get divorced.
- The studies haven't yet examined the long-term stats of the new generation of live-in couples.
- The studies are all-encompassing. Factors other than just living together, including socioeconomic trends, can affect people's relationships greatly.
- We are not a statistic, you (insert descriptive noun of your choosing)!

Still deciding whether to move in with him? Ask yourself these questions before taking the plunge.

- Why am I moving in with him—is it a good enough reason to take such a big step?
- What are my expectations about a future with him? Have I talked this over with him in detail? Is he on the same page?
- If I'm expecting to someday marry him, how long am I expecting to be shacking up first? How long is he anticipating?
- When/how will we decide whether the living situation is working or not?
- What if one of us changes our mind about marriage?
- How will I deal with people who don't think we should be living together?
- How well do he and I communicate?

- How do our arguments normally go? Do we both fight in a healthy, nonabusive way? Have we had our first big blowout argument yet?
- Can I share my possessions with this person?
- What are his living habits like? Do I think he and I can make splitting up household chores work?
- Will he treat me with respect at all times?
- Will I be able to change and grow with him at my side? What if he changes as well—will I still feel the same way about him?
- Is he supportive of me and my goals?
- What would we do if he/I lost his/my job? Or if one of us decided to change career paths?
- What forms of birth control are we using? What if I got pregnant?
- What will happen if we break up?

Read Read Read

Go ahead, keep reading! After all, you hold in your hands this guide to help you navigate the wild world of living in sin . . . er . . . living with your boyfriend. We'll cover everything from dealing with your families to keeping things romantic. From decorating the place to splitting up day-to-day chores. We'll not only give you tips to help you through the experience successfully, but also to make it fun!

Be warned: Each chapter starts off with a real problem or obstacle a woman has faced during cohabitation in order to help you with similar issues should they arise. The tips you'll find are straight from the mouths of women who've survived cohabitation. Some are now married, some have split up, and others are still cohabiting. No matter the outcome, they seriously know what they're talking about—who better to advise you?

The names and/or identifying information of some of the women quoted in this book were changed at their request. We don't think they were embarrassed or anything. We just figured they'd dish more juicy details if their boyfriends, mothers, and boyfriends' mothers would never find out. And they did.

1.

legal issues and domestic partnerships

I had an ex-boyfriend, after five years, just up and leave, as if our life together never existed. The apartment situation was tough. To make ends meet, I had to rent out my bedroom and move into my living room until my lease was up five months later. It was weird to be a stranger in my own apartment. As for the stuff he left behind, I threw it out. Seven months later, he asked for his share of the deposit back. I told him he was crazy and didn't deserve anything, and that I didn't have anything to give him. Fortunately, his abrupt departure had made me hate him enough to move on.

—Nikki, fashion designer, Los Angeles

We know you're completely giddy and gaga over this guy. Breaking up is the last thing on your mind right now, and so is the scenario where one of you gets sick, goes to war, needs dental insurance, or the like. We're not trying to snap you out of your sappy state (because, really, we find it far more cute than icky) but it can't hurt to know what your legal rights are as a couple that's not married and also to protect yourself in the event that you don't live happily ever after.

Let's start from square one: Where will you live and what will the arrangement be? Whether you've chosen to live in a place where one of you lives now or you are finding a new place together, be sure both of you have your name on the lease, deeded title, or sublet agreement. We know, we know; he has better credit than you, or you have to bug your landlord to change the paperwork you already have in place (you might even have to pay a lawyer to draw up the papers—or a find a notary to make it official). But, seriously, lady. Just do it.

Marin Feldman, an attorney with a legal firm in New York City, suggests, "Even though having both your names on the lease is a double-edged sword, your best bet is to get on it. What happens when you put both names on the lease is that you and your boyfriend are both jointly and separately liable for the lease. In other words, your landlord can go after either one of you to collect the full rent. However, if you don't sign the lease, your boyfriend has the legal right to kick you out at any time."

Feldman suggests, "You could try to have a separate provision put in your lease that says each of you is liable for half the rent. But few landlords are likely to go for that. Another option you have is to have a third party come on as a guarantor. Maybe your boyfriend has a rich father or aunt. The rent itself still falls to you as far as the landlord is concerned. But then you are able to sue the guarantor in the event that your boyfriend bails on rent."

Bottom line? Having both of your names on official paperwork not only gives you a leg to stand on if—and we're not saying it's going to happen—you guys break up, but it's also important for your own personal use down the line. For example, when you get your driver's license, or have it renewed, you'll likely need proof of your address. When you want to buy a car, they're going to run a credit check. If you've been responsible with your mortgage payments, your credit will look good. If you don't have your name on a mortgage, depending on other factors, you might not get the credit score you need to get the car loan. These don't sound like a big deal? Well, they become a big deal when you spend hours at the dealership negotiating the price on that brand-new cherry-red flatbed truck—then they finally give in and give you the deal and the papers must be signed posthaste!

Famous Relationships that Started Good, Ended Badly

- Romeo and Juliet
  Dude, killing yourselves is not the answer.
- Scarlett and Rhett
  He may have stopped giving a damn just when she was ready to come around. How's that for crappy timing?
- John and Lorena Bobbitt
  You probably know the . . . um . . . long and short of it.
- Jennifer Aniston and Brad Pitt
  They were so cute together. But come on, compete against Angie? That body and a United Nations Ambassador?
- Britney Spears and Kevin Federline
  Actually, we take that back. That was never good and we all knew it.

The fact is, with your name on documents comes financial power and freedom. For things you share, like cars, bills, or boats (and if you have a boat, we should definitely hang out some time), try to get both names on record, or stagger whose name is on what. Let's just say that you don't want to get stuck paying for everything, and you want to be able to prove that you've paid for things in the past.

TIPS FOR PUTTING YOUR NAME ON BILLS AND LOANS

Share ownership on completely shared items like a car you each drive 50 percent of the time, if that's the case.

Stagger "ownership" of smaller bills (his name is on the electricity bill, yours is on the phone bill), so you both can prove you make payments and that you share responsibility.

If you use something 75 percent of the time, your name should be on it. And vice versa.

If he is bad at making payments on time, make sure your name is not on the bills he pays. Late payments hurt the credit of the account holder, no matter who the screwup is.

It's always easier to make sure that each of you has ownership of the proper items in the beginning, instead of later in front of a judge. Try to prevent problems from the beginning.

Believe us, you want this. You drive the Miata more often? Your name should be on it. In fact, Tara, an architect from Baltimore, made sure her name was on all the utility bills when she moved in with her guy. "I'm a control freak. I want to be in charge of the bills, and I don't trust anyone else to be in charge of my credit but me," she says.

But avoid taking the responsibility for possessions you don't want to pay for. If he begs you to put your name on the Harley because you have a better credit score and can get a better rate for the loan, think twice about it. If you won't be making payments and won't be using the bike—and for that matter, hate the noise it will make—tell him you'd feel more comfortable if it's only in his name. This way, if he misses payments, it will only hurt his credit, and if something happens

between the two of you, it's his future responsibility, not yours. Plus, you won't have to go through the whole process of changing the name on the title. For some reason, the DMV makes that more of a pain in the ass than it really should be. We know. The DMV a pain in the ass? Never!

Jackie Gutter, an attorney practicing Domestic Law in Columbus, Ohio, concurs. "Don't put his name on the title of your car. In fact, make sure you remain very clear about what you own," says Gutter. "Because you are not married, no one has more legal rights over the other. In cases involving marital property, if a couple can't reach a mutual decision about property, they can usually make a case for themselves if it goes to trial. Things are very cut and dry when a couple is married because almost all marital property is mutually owned. It is more complicated if you are unmarried. So the more proof you have that something belongs to you, the better off you are. Save receipts and put your name on leases and titles."

At the end of the day, which fight would you rather have: the one where he pouts for a few hours because he didn't get his way? Or the one where you are trying to hold together every ounce of remaining dignity in front of Judge Wapner? Yeah. That's what we thought, too.

Landlord vs. Tenant

So, which is it—buying or renting? If you haven't decided yet, you're going to have to make a pro and con list depending on your own personal needs. We're going to help you weigh your options and let you know the right way to do it.

La Vie Boheme

Renting is the most common arrangement for the women we polled. Why? As Amber, a physician in Beaver Falls, Pennsylvania, puts it, "It's an opportunity to see how well you can handle bills and finances together before you jump into buying." Let's face it, renting instead of buying is a bit like cohabiting instead of getting married—less commitment involved. You are usually only in it for a year, and then you're free to make changes or carry on. As we mentioned before, it's important that you're both on the lease, or at least that there's some sort of sublet agreement between you two. You want documentation that you're both financially responsible if someone wants out of the lease at an inopportune moment. You might also agree on how to split up the security deposit in the end—and have contingency options depending on how things do go down in the end (or up—we are not pessimists!) of the relationship.

"I know of a woman who had a place, and her boyfriend moved in—he was unemployed," says Emily, a teacher in Chicago. "She paid for everything; he mooched. He then flooded the place by leaving the washing machine on or something, broke up with her, moved out and left her stuck, not only with a flooded apartment, but with the downstairs neighbor's flooded apartment below it."

REASONS TO MAKE SURE YOU'RE BOTH ON THE LEASE

You're both liable for the lease and outstanding payments if you break up.

Legally, neither of you can kick the other out—even in the heat of an argument.

You'll both have proof of your address for purposes such as getting a driver's license or parking permit.

On the other hand, most of the women we asked about this were more like Brianne, a sales rep in Kansas City: "It all comes down to trust," she says. "I trust my boyfriend to be an adult and handle things maturely if we were to break up. Now I could be totally naive, but if I didn't believe he was a stand-up guy, why the hell did I move in with him in the first place?" Really, just to be sure, though: other than a small fee you might incur, there's no reason he should refuse you both being on the lease. Don't be afraid to insist. You are woman—you can roar, you know.

Buy, Buy Baby

Buying is a whole different football game. There are plenty of reasons to buy a home—you're not throwing away money on rent, you're building equity, you might even make a profit when you sell, you can paint the walls cherry red if you want, and you don't have to live with hospital-tiled-looking bathrooms. But remember that a home is most people's largest asset, their investment toward the future. If you share it with a guy with whom your future is ambiguous, perhaps you are putting the cart before the horse. We know that just because you are not married does not mean you are not committed, but this is one of those times to get really clear with each other about where you are in your relationship. If you are prepared to invest in a future together, buying is a great option. But if you are dipping your toe into a potential future together at this point, maybe rent for a year first.

There are plenty of things to consider—and we're talking about covering your ass, because you know Murphy's Law, right? If it can go wrong, it will. For starters, decide where the down payment will come from. Will you share the responsibility of coming up with it, or will one of you be hitting up a rich uncle? How can you protect that investment?

"You don't necessarily need a lawyer from the get-go," says Feldman. "You just want to make sure both your and his names are on the deed no matter who makes the down payment. There is something called the Statute of Frauds that dictates that any conveyance of land or real property has to be in writing."

She goes on to caution, "Chances are most jurisdictions will recognize your deed as a Tenants in Common deed since you are unmarried. This is a good thing, so double-check before the deed is issued. This way, if you make the down payment and then you break up, the deed will have been partitioned by sale. In other words, you will have split ownership of the house based on a percentage. You will therefore be entitled to your deposit back plus any money that later goes into the property. Again, just make sure your percentage of ownership is in writing."

"Now if you have bad credit, say," she continues, "and he goes on the deed by himself because you couldn't otherwise get the sale, and you make the down payment, be aware that it is going to be really hard, nearly impossible, to convince any court that you

PROS OF BUYING A HOME
Ideally, you get your monthly payments back when you sell.
You build equity.
Real estate often appreciates. Profits are good!
You can make home improvements.
You can totally split ownership of a home.

CONS OF BUYING A HOME
Buying a home takes almost as much commitment as marriage. It takes time to build equity in a house and for its value to appreciate.
You'll need to cover your ass a little: one buyer's name on a deed means the other has few to no rights.
Breaking up would probably mean having to sell the place.
You could end up as co-landlords if you break up and can't sell the place.

should be paid back. It will likely be considered a gift and you will be considered a trespasser if he wants you to leave. In this case, you should make sure he signs a promissory note that would make your down payment more like a loan. It should indicate that the amount will be paid back in the event that you leave the residence.

MOVING IN MANTRA: ON MONEY

"I have never been in a situation where having money made it worse."—CLINTON JONE

Some promissory notes expire after six years, so keep that in mind as well." Renee and her former live-in boyfriend had some trouble selling their place when they broke up, so now they're renting it out. "We had to accept that we were going to have to be co-landlords," she says. Remember that this could conceivably happen to you—consider how both of you would handle it.

We Still Wish Money Grew on Trees

Now that we've got the big stuff out of the way, consider all the little stuff that adds up: phone bills, insurance payments, gas and electricity—you know, all those lovely envelopes that are delivered so unfailingly to your mailbox every month? And on top of that, costs like food, cleaning products, movie rentals, and even those awesome Fro-Yo bonbons you love to eat on Friday nights.

Christy Calame, a licensed clinical social worker and relationship expert with over ten years' experience in couples therapy in Oakland, California, points out, "Money in particular evokes emotions that are learned throughout your life. It brings up powerful stuff like anxiety and, in some cases, terror."

So, when it comes to money, the more plans you have in place the better equipped you will be when figuring out how to cope with it in your relationship. Documentation is good, too: as a precaution, Feldman emphasizes that it is really important to keep track of all major household spending. "Document the source of all funds you spend," she says. "Write them down anywhere, even on the checks themselves so they can be traced."

Our best advice is to split the cost of everything down the middle. Obviously it's the fair way and it usually makes the most sense—a lot of couples find it to be the easiest way to avoid arguments about who is contributing more. Of course, unless you take every bill and every grocery receipt and nickel and dime each other to death, how you split it up exactly is totally up to you.

"If he wrote the utilities checks, then I would pay for the groceries, and so on," explains Hope. "Everything seemed to naturally even out even though we never actually wrote two equal checks for anything other than groceries." An arrangement like Hope's can totally work out for you. Just be sure that you and he are on the same page when it comes to the ways each of you can contribute. It might be a good idea to create an Excel spreadsheet of your monthly financial commitments and make a plan that seems as even as possible.

Georgia, a civil engineer in Tampa, Florida, found success splitting the bills another way. "We both put our money in a joint account. All bills were paid from that account," she says. "Savings accounts that we had prior were kept separate."

Proceed with extreme caution here. Having a joint account means you both have access to each other's money. This may not

---

IDEAS FOR PAYING THE BILLS AND KEEPING THINGS FAIR

Split everything right down the middle—write two separate checks for it all.

Take turns paying for things.

List everything you pay for in a month, and divide up the bills in the most even way possible.

If you completely trust each other, you can each put an even amount in a joint account and pay the bills from that account.

work if one of you is a spender and the other is a saver. Make certain you are in agreement about your relationship when deciding to open a joint account. While we are behind you 100 percent if you want to move in together because it's convenient and you both enjoy Parcheesi, we can't say that the same casual attitude applies to mingling your bank accounts!

But sometimes splitting *everything* down the middle might not be in both your best interests. Like when one of you consumes quite a bit more than the other. Take the example of Kim, an English and humanities teacher in Columbus, Ohio. Her ex-boyfriend could really eat. Says Kim: "Sure, we shared. But I didn't eat leftovers for almost two years. I would come home and the fridge would look like a ghost town . . . Sometimes I felt like I was dating one giant gullet with feet, like I was slipping my paychecks down that big throat."

WHAT EXPENSES SHOULD BE KEPT SEPARATE BY AN UNMARRIED COUPLE
Any service or item one of you uses and the other doesn't
Cell phone bills
Credit card bills
Checking accounts, usually
Savings accounts
Personal items like clothing, sports equipment, etc.
Student loans
Business expenses

If you find yourself in a similar situation to Kim, the direct approach is probably best. Ask him to pitch in more for groceries—or to be the one to buy that pricey French caviar he loves so much that makes you want to gag. The simple idea that the one who eats more should pay more could prove, well, priceless.

Remember that there are certain things that should probably remain separately your expenses or his expenses. Like that motorcycle we mentioned—or even little things. "We each have our own cell phones and credit cards," says Serena, a dance teacher in Oak Park, Illinois. "And we have separate bank accounts, which I love, because once the bills are paid, we can do what we want with what's left. I don't get on his case for buying a new golf bag, and he can't say anything if I buy new shoes."

Things like student loans, business expenses, and that gorgeous Louis Vuitton bag you have to have are probably best kept separate. You don't want to get into the situation where one of you has to ask the other for permission to take a taxi instead of the bus or something of the sort.

Come On! Pay the Piper

Now what if either one of you makes significantly more than the other—or there's just one breadwinner? The fact is, it isn't unusual for one half of a couple to earn more than the other. So how do you handle the tension that may come up when one of you is managing more bills than the other? What's important is that you're open with each other about your responsibilities and that you're both making an effort to keep each other's best interests in mind.

Christine, a fashion designer in Manhattan, made a deal with her boyfriend Gabe, a businessman who made a lot more money than she did. "I became agreeably domestic," she says. "I took care of the household and most meals. We were clear about it and Gabe knew that even though he paid a lot more of the rent and for most of our going-out expenses, I would be responsible for getting bills paid and keeping things clean. But I paid for the cat that he was allergic to and, of course, my own personal items."

In other words, make sure you're supporting each other. Maybe one of you can't compare to the other financially right now, but you're pitching in in other amazing ways. The feeling that you're not contributing, or that your partner is not contributing, can cause major rifts in your relationship.

However, one of you might be a student or unemployed or waiting for an old rich relative to die while the other is providing the income for you both temporarily. In a case like this, be clear with each other about whether this constitutes a loan that will be paid back once the other has gotten back on his or her feet—or if it is all household money that keeps you living in the manner to which you are accustomed. In this case, it makes sense to discuss every purchase made, to be sure the breadwinner agrees with the other's choice.

Of course, not everything has to be formally agreed upon. "He was broke," says June, a filmmaker in Brooklyn. "So I never expected him to pay me back for cable. I knew that if it was just him, he never would have had it. And I was not about to give it up."

If you are like Lisa, a consultant in Bloomfield, New Jersey, your commitment might transcend money. "We kinda knew we were in it for the long haul," she explains. "When we moved in, we split rent down the middle. I think we were pretty fast and loose with the groceries. CDs were

STRATEGIES FOR COUPLES WITH DISPARITIES IN INCOME
If it's an issue, make up for a significantly lower income with other household contributions, like cooking or cleaning.
Keep elective expenses like clothing separate so you each can regulate your spending.
If one of you has a temporary lack of funds, put any "loans" in writing.
Discuss big purchases, and if there's only one breadwinner, discuss *every* purchase until some things are just understood.
If there's something you want and he doesn't, pay for it. Same goes for him.

strictly 'mine' and 'yours.' I bought the couch myself. But once we got engaged, we just went to strictly 'ours.'"

Hey, that's pretty romantic!

Naked Soccer Studs

So, if you are one of those people who hears the word "Law" in a title and starts to doze off, we have decided *not* to title this segment "What Is a Common-Law Marriage?" Wow, how completely fun does this part of the chapter sound? But the thing is, it's kind of totally and unequivocally vital to every choice you have made, will make, or are making!

As Laura, a director in Pittsburgh, Pennsylvania, brilliantly observes, "You should know if you are in a common-law state or if your state makes any assumption regarding your legal status together. Know this for certain because there are many things that can be impacted if your state thinks you are legally bound and declares your assets to be mutually owned."

Laura goes on to mention that in the event of a divorce, savings accounts and even retirement plans can come up for grabs. She's right. Grandma's wedding ring and that Volkswagen you paid off

COMMON-LAW MARRIAGE IS RECOGNIZED IN THESE STATES
Alabama
Colorado
District of Columbia
Georgia (if created before 1/1/97)
Idaho (if created before 1/1/96)
Iowa
Kansas
Montana
New Hampshire (for inheritance purposes only)
Ohio (if created before 10/10/91)
Oklahoma
Pennsylvania
Rhode Island
South Carolina
Texas
Utah

are things you absolutely don't want to split down the middle. If you simply bat your adorable eyelashes and say "But I never said *I do . . .*" you might find a judge innocently batting eyelashes right back at you going "But you may as well have." It is for the protection of both of you. Do your research.

To clarify, in most cases you *don't* enter into a common-law marriage by simply living together. *Phew!* However, if you often refer to each other as "husband" or "wife" and make the general claim that you are married—further, if your widely known intention is to be married and you file your taxes jointly—the argument for common-law marriage can be readily made.

Feldman, our legal expert, assures us, "It is really hard to unwittingly get married. In other words, you can't accidentally find yourself married just because you keep going back to the same Chinese restaurant together every Sunday. You both have to pretty much agree to being married or to choosing to present yourselves as married."

COMMON-LAW "MARRIAGE" FACTS
Your assets may be mutually owned.
If you break up, you may have to fight for the money in your savings account, 401(k), trust fund, and more.
You live in a "common-law state."
You have lived together a certain number of years.
You probably have claimed that you are married or referred to each other as "husband" and "wife."
You probably file your taxes jointly.

Delicious Chocolate Dripping off Sweet Strawberries

This particular section is also known as What are Domestic Partners All About? Well, clearly they are unmarried couples who live, er, *domestically* under one roof. Unlike with common-law marriages—or, in this country, real-life marriages—Domestic Partnerships can involve same-sex couples, as they were in many cases created by gay and lesbian organizations fighting for legal rights.

The rules for Domestic Partnerships vary from state to state, so it is really important that you look into exactly what yours are.

Typically, Domestic Partnerships are dictated by the state as well as the policies of an employer. You should look into protocol, such as how a couple should register, whether or not a couple qualifies only if they are the same sex or whether they can be opposite-sex partners. Look into how many years you need to be together as a couple and what your financial responsibility to each other must be. Find this information in your employee handbook or call your human resources department.

DOMESTIC PARTNERSHIPS INCLUDE SOME VERSION OF THESE BENEFITS
Health, dental, and vision insurance
Sick and bereavement leave
Accident and life insurance
Death benefits
Parental leave (for a child you co-parent)
Housing rights and tuition reduction (at universities)
Use of recreational facilities

"To become Domestic Partners you have to file," says legal expert Jackie Gutter. "There are forms you can find online or through your human resources department at work. They will tell you exactly what you need to prove that you are more than just roommates. Often you must share a checking account and share a lease. Your proof must then be notarized."

Understand that once you have become Domestic Partners, while the benefits of his health care covering your acupuncture is a bonus, you become more entwined in each other's lives. Feldman points out, "Rights can include health insurance, hospital visitation, inheritance. Sometimes all, sometimes one." Find out exactly what that entails, and make sure that you are ready to leave your 401(k) to this guy if you get hit by a bus. It might be in his rights even if you had only wanted him to be your "in case of emergency" person.

In some cases, filing for Domestic Partnership makes sense because the two of you are completely comfortable with a deeper commitment. In other cases, the fact that you didn't marry each other was probably for a reason. So continue reading ways to protect yourself when you are not ready to invite Uncle Sam, Jesus, or his mother into your relationship with your man, just a lease.

Just a Lease, Not a Law

There are ways to protect yourself. Some are complex and involve lawyers or people otherwise wearing bad hairpieces. Others are simpler.

If anyone has stayed home sick from work or school, they have watched a judge show (you know, Judy, Wapner, Joe Brown . . . we know we're not the only ones). Weird as it sounds, you can write up a "legal" agreement—it can even be in crayon—and with such written documentation, you can win in small claims court. "Courts will usually uphold almost any cohabitation agreements," says Feldman. You could go to the trouble of writing up a formal "prenup" to protect your assets in case of a breakup. Seriously, you can, even if you're not getting married. But as Lindsey, a magazine writer in Brooklyn, eloquently put it, "I have never heard of a 'cohabitation prenup' but I think it sounds atrocious. What kind

Drafting a Domestic Partnership Agreement

According to an article published in 2005 by Forbes magazine, a great way to create a financial structure in your household is to write up a domestic partnership agreement. Each of you gets a copy for your records. Later, this document is enforceable in a small claims court, or a higher court depending on how much is at stake, in the event of a breakup. Use the following tips to draft your own version:

1. Keep it simple. Too many bells and whistles could take the wind out of the sails of your relationship. It isn't supposed to be the reason for the breakup!
2. State that all personal property brought into the household will leave with the person it arrived with.
3. Even if one person earns more than the other, it still may be best to say that expenses will be split fifty-fifty with the higher earner paying more to be paid back once the other person is able. In this case, keep a careful record of all expenses. If you agree that the higher earner will pay more, put a figure to it. In other words, he will pay 80 percent of all household necessities and you will pay 20 percent. Just keep it clear and whenever possible, attach a value. For example, if your rent is $1000, he will pay $800 and you will pay the remaining $200.
4. State that you will seek the help of a moderator in the event of a breakup after which expenses cannot be equitably split. In other words, you'll ask for help if you can't hash out on your own who owes for cable when you weren't the one watching the pay-per-view porn.
5. Make it clear who gets to keep the house, and come up with provisions for the cat, the hula dancer lamp, and the Styrofoam finger collection.

All of this goes out the window when children are involved, in which case we advise you to get a lawyer and know your rights.

of person needs something like that? I think it's ridiculous and totally unnecessary."

Still, while it sounds totally unromantic, it may feel like the right thing for *you* to do. What you might not have thought of is protecting yourself—after all, doesn't falling in love with someone mean you have to let your guard down a *lot*? The thing to remember here is, while you guys may be all honeysuckle and rose gardens right now, breakups are rarely pretty. The fact is, Dylan and Brenda totally faked staying friends on 90210 back in the early '90s, especially when he started dating Kelly, which was made clear when Bren left for Europe without so much as a goodbye a few seasons later. And there are more horror stories out there. But we digress.

"The fact is, prenups aren't sexy but they work," says Feldman. "It's like a condom: it might take some passion out of the moment but later on, you're sure glad you used it!"

As Lisa points out, "A cohabitation 'prenup' might be a good idea if you have a lot on the line, like a child, a house, or a sizable amount of money or goods." When stuff is involved, you can imagine how messy it can all get. Suddenly, it is your pissed-off word against his that the sofa was your great grandmother's and that you never promised it to him in exchange for his hanging the toilet paper holder in the bathroom. The thing is, your pissed-off word against his is way less fun than it sounds. And it don't sound fun. If a cohabitation prenup is something you're interested in, look up a lawyer in the yellow pages and discuss it with her.

Of course, you might not have anything worth protecting, like Lindsey, who says, "We have no plan for a potential breakup, but I'm sure we would split up the mutual things, like furniture.

SHOULD YOU HAVE A COHABITATION "PRENUP"?

Do I have any significant assets, like a home or a car?

How much do I trust him if we break up?

Do I have children to protect?

Is there any other possession I never want to risk parting with?

Will it really hurt my relationship if I make him put it in writing?

However, neither of us is too attached to any of it! We found most of it on the street, so we might just put it back where it came from." Colleen, a translator in Amsterdam, concurred. "Regarding material belongings, the last thing you want to do is argue over a piece of furniture at the end of the day. I'm sure by that point I'd just be like, fuck it, take it. I'm moving on."

We still say, grab a crayon and write down what's yours—we're talking big-ticket items and stuff with sentimental value. Sign it. Get him drunk and make him sign it, then put it away. Let's just say, it can't hurt.

Q & A with a Legal Expert

Jackie Gutter, an attorney practicing domestic law in Columbus, Ohio, answers some touchy legal questions.

Q: *I want to make sure that, in an emergency, he'd be the one to get a phone call and make decisions when I can't—not my parents, who live out of town. How can I do that?*

A: "There is no formal way of becoming someone's 'in case of emergency' person. Just add the person's name to whatever forms you are filling out on which the question comes up. This includes your file in your company's human resources department, and the ones you fill out in the doctor's office.

"In Intensive Care cases where only family is allowed to visit, most places do informally let anyone in. But in the long run, the best thing to do is to get a power of attorney for health care. That way you can appoint your partner to make important health decisions on your behalf. You could also consider a living will, which would work in much the same way as far as indicating your wishes should you become unable to communicate them. Do a search online to find the paperwork for this—you'll probably need to have it notarized and keep it in a safe place."

Q: *We're thinking about sharing health insurance. When is that a good idea, and when is it not?*

A. "The cost of being put on your partner's insurance can often determine which insurance policy to go on. Some policies don't increase rates for adding a domestic partner. If there are costs for adding a partner, you might want to split these costs or pass them off entirely, especially if your insurance is your partner's only way to become insured. The likelihood is that being added to someone else's policy will be far far less expensive than obtaining a private insurance policy, which are almost always very expensive.

"However, you might want to avoid claiming domestic partnership or getting married if one of you is unwell and insured through Medicaid. Otherwise the income of both parties is accounted for and you might lose your benefits if collectively you earn more than is allowed by Medicaid. Adding and removing a domestic partner to an insurance policy is fairly easy to do. If the policy is yours through work, often it takes little more than a phone call to your provider to add or remove someone from your policy."

Q: *Can we get separate renter's or homeowner's insurance policies?*

A: "It may not be possible to obtain more than one insurance policy since only one place is being insured. You can always look into getting a larger policy once there are two of you living in the space. The same goes for homeowner's insurance. Two policies might be impossible to get. But an increase in the size of the policy makes sense. Make sure your name is on the policy to ensure that even in a messy breakup, you are entitled to a payout.

"Homeowner's insurance obviously covers a lot more than renter's insurance. After all, a landlord is responsible for all that a renter is not."

Q: *What about car insurance?*

A: "Normally it is the car that is insured. If you both drive the car equally it is a good idea to have both your names on the insurance. But you are not required by law to do so. The fact is, if your rates go up because someone else crashes you car, there's not much you can do about it, no matter whose name is on the insurance. So be careful about who you let drive it!"

2.

family and societal issues

My dad doesn't like the fact that we're "living in sin" and thinks it shows [that my boyfriend] disrespects me. I understand that his views are outdated and patriarchal, but it's still disconcerting sometimes to know that he is so upset and there's nothing I can do to change his mind. When we discuss it I sound like a broken record, and so does he!

—Lindsey

Okay, so we've established that some might say you two are living in sin. The good news is, being sinful is cool, mainstream, modern, the opposite of boring. Elvis's "sinful" hip gyrations won him platinum records. Johnny Rotten claimed to be the Antichrist. Sinning has practically grown wings. It has become the new black. Even ice cream is now described as "sinful"—and it's hard to deny, ice cream is *good*.

But let's face it, while it's cool to be a sinner in a punk rock band, in real life things get a bit more complicated. The dictionary defines a sin as a "transgression of divine law." And that's heavy. It comes down to things like fire and brimstone.

If you bought this book, you're either already living with your boyfriend or thinking about it, so we're guessing that you don't find that cohabitation conflicts with your religious beliefs. But maybe it conflicts with someone else's: your parents', your grandmother's, your nosy neighbor's. Unfortunately for some people in our otherwise open-minded, nonjudgmental culture, you might find yourself doing a lot of 'splainin' to people you never thought you'd have to 'splain yourself to in a post-MTV world. Unfortunately, moving in with a boyfriend can cut straight to the heart of much deeper issues encompassing everything from spirituality to propriety. For the same reason people who look at porn magazines tend not to display them on their coffee tables, parents whose children cohabit might wish they wouldn't flaunt it. And they'll come right out and say so.

For Lee, a yoga instructor in Boston, Massachusetts, it was her mother's church community that made the idea of cohabitation so completely out of the question. "If I wanted a relationship with my mother, Chris was going to have to put a ring on my finger. I don't know if Jesus had as much to do with it as the gossipy ladies from my mom's church group."

Yes, sometimes it is your faith against theirs.

"There are a lot of reasons not to get married," says Sharon, a science teacher in Pittsburgh, "and a lot of reasons to move in together. That's just what I believe."

So what happens when you believe in moving in without the ring and they don't?

Well, one option is to flat-out lie. Hini, a lawyer from West Virginia, opted out of telling her parents when she moved in with Eli. It seemed to be going pretty well, since they lived far away and rarely had the chance to visit. But after two years, they figured it out. "I screwed up with the mail," she admits. "I never told my parents I had moved from my old apartment and one day my mom mailed me something. It was returned to her and she confronted me."

A lot of parents and grandparents are against cohabitation because it's an unfamiliar concept to them, since it wasn't as much an option when they were young.

"We started living together in Minneapolis in 1980," says Karen, a consultant who now lives with her husband and two kids in New Jersey. "We were living in one apartment and wanted something larger than what we had, so Howard was looking at other places. While he was talking with a landlord about the 'friend' he'd be moving there with, the landlord realized he was referring to his girlfriend, and that we weren't married. The landlord said, 'My wife doesn't approve of that.' His wife, stone-faced and arms crossed, stood next to him glaring at Howard. We didn't get that apartment."

Ten Things You Might Not Want to Say To Your Disapproving Parents

1. "Get with the times."
2. "You guys don't know him like I do because you haven't gotten conjugal visits like I have over the last year!"
3. "We had to get a new mattress. The old one's springs were getting worn out."
4. "Just *look* at how hot he is!"
5. "But my sister did it!" (Never out the siblings . . .)
6. "Seriously, he makes fabulous breakfast burritos."

7. "It isn't like you guys are saints. I found mom's pasties."
8. "But his whip collection totally complements my S&M video collection!"
9. "But everyone else is doing it!"
10. "I don't know his last name, but when I met him at the supermarket last week, I could just tell that we were soul mates."

Rebel Yell

Being afraid to tell your parents about your moving-in plans, or in some cases your having-already-moved-in plans, isn't the most unheard-of thing in the world. Seeking parental approval is human and often deeply rooted. And in many cases, people discover that they have underestimated their parents' open-mindedness.

Amanda, a graphic designer in San Francisco, California, says, "Marc was terrified to tell his parents because they are pastors and frown upon living together before marriage. They accepted it fine, though, and were more concerned that Marc had been uncomfortable communicating his decision to them."

Still, err on the safe side. As with any delicate information, it is best to avoid blurting it out or waiting until stressful moments. In other words, your announcement should not come when you are pissed off at your mom for criticizing your new hairstyle. "It is important to consider intentionality and timing," says our relationship expert Christy Calame. "Think of it as a 'coming out' process."

"We told my parents over dinner. We announced it like an engagement," says Tina, a fashion designer from Ontario, Canada. This is a fantastic idea.

Present the plan in the same spirit in which it was conceived to make it easier for your parents to process. Don't act like you are

MOVING-IN MANTRA: ON RELIGION

"It is a fine thing to establish one's own religion in one's heart, not to be dependent on tradition and second-hand ideals. Life will seem to you, later, not a lesser, but a greater thing."—D. H. LAWRENCE

doing something wrong. No shifting your weight or acting like you are admitting to . . . well, sinning. Keep it positive. Explain to your parents how you see this move. If it is simply a financial one, say so. If it is a decision you are clear and confident about making, it won't be impossible to show them why. Point out what is good and safe about your relationship and why the step is the right one for the two of you. Even if you aren't sure he is forever, make it clear to those would-be naysayers why you are sure he is the right one right now. It is best to have these ideas sussed out before sitting everyone down. But allow for conversation—and some time for acceptance.

"Have patience. It might happen in stages," says Calame. "There might be more than one point of communication. In other words, you might need to start with a talk. If you suspect this talk should be in person, do it in person. If it is better for you to do it over the phone, do it over the phone. Next you might follow it up with a letter and then another conversation, after everyone has had some time to digest it."

In the end make sure you ask them how they will be most comfortable dealing with your new arrangement. Then try to respect their boundaries.

"I agreed to accept my mother's dislike for the situation, and I accepted that she wasn't coming over for dinner or buying us a housewarming gift," says Joy, a photographer from Idaho. "I drew the line at lying. She wanted me to lie to my grandmother but I refused."

As in any relationship that is important to us, we have to respect different points of view, but ultimately, it is your life and your decisions are yours. Own them.

Great Strategies for Lying

We're not saying that fibbing to your folks is right. But if you have your mind made up to do it, this is what we recommend:

1. Have as little contact with them as possible. There is a trade off for lying. You won't have to deal with the nasty fights but you will have to cut down on family dinners.
2. Practice. Start off with small lies ("Dean lives across town.") and then work your way up ("Why did he answer my phone at 8:00 in the morning, you ask? Well we've started to practice yoga sun salutations every Wednesday at 7:30 a.m., and he comes over for that. You called just as we were finishing up. I'm feeling very Zen right now.").
3. Use details. But remember what they are. Write them down in one place that you keep in a hiding spot your parents will never find.
4. Believe your lie. When in the presence of your grandmother you don't even *have* a boyfriend, much less live with one.
5. You must think about to whom you will be telling your story, and why they would believe you.
6. Make sure you both have the same story in case you get caught.

7. Always be ready with excuses and if you are asked for more details, have that information.

8. The last thing to remember: if anyone asks, stick to the same story. *Never* make up two lies about the same incident. Even when your mom is holding his razor full of bright red hair, inevitably a by-product of his Irish ancestry and not your Cambodian one, the only thing to say is: "What do you mean, 'Is this John's?' Do I even know a John?"

Tradition!

Let's face it. The bottom line on this is that most organized religions, especially in the Judeo-Christian models, forbid cohabitation. To begin with, there's the whole modesty thing, the-thou-shalt-not-own-sex-toys-or-lacey-underwear-or-pee-in-front-of-a-man-who-isn't-your-husband thing.

If you truly believe these ideas, be careful about compromising them. As Rachael, a wedding planner in Crested

HOW TO TELL MOM AND DAD

Avoid bringing it up during a stressful or emotional situation.

Consider timing: we recommend making an official announcement over dinner or otherwise in person when a discussion can then be invited.

Present it in a positive way: explain your excitement and loving feelings toward him. Be honest about why you're moving in together.

Tell them why you're confident you're making the right decision.

Point out the good things about your relationship with him and why he's the right one right now.

Allow for conversation—listen to their side of the story, but ultimately tell them you've made up your mind.

Give them some time to accept your decision.

If they don't accept it right away, follow up later with another conversation, or even a phone call or note.

Try to respect their opinion, but ultimately do what's right for you.

Remember that they may be more open-minded than you think.

Butte, Colorado, explained about moving in with her boyfriend, "It was just easier." She went on to admit "I think it probably weakened my ethics and self-esteem." Use her experience as a lesson: be sure you know why you moved in together and know how your domestic situation strengthens your own beliefs and values.

Speaking with a member of the clergy might be a really good way for you to explore your feelings on the matter. But for the most part, try not to choose someone whose reply you can anticipate. In other words, don't pick the crazy hippie Rabbi because you want the definite yes, or find yourself in debate with the ultra-chaste nun who is a guaranteed no. You might actually be surprised how understanding the minister or monk you grew up with can actually be. Just because the literal doctrine frowns upon cohabitation doesn't mean you're forever damned for doing it. In fact, we believe, when done right, it is a great and wonderful thing to do!

If you fear that a particular life choice will compromise your spiritual beliefs, you might find it is difficult to decide what to do. Ask yourself if it would make you feel more secure in your decision if you modified your religious practices in other ways.

religions that support cohabitation

Buddhism: The greatest action is not conforming with the world's ways.
Wicca: "I look at the overall spectrum of the universe and see patterns within every walk in life past and present, and therefore avoid unnecessary and outdated limitations."—The Eclectic Witch
Unitarian Universalism: The name "Universalism" originated with the belief in "universal" salvation, the idea that everyone will be saved and no one is eternally damned.
Satanism: Dude, we think the Devil will let you live with your boyfriend.

MOVING-IN MANTRA: ON COMMUNICATING

"The single biggest problem in communication is the illusion that it has taken place."—GEORGE BERNARD SHAW

Like what if you increased the number of times per year you go to some service? Or what if you make a point once a day or week (or okay, every third month) to meditate or pray? If you don't already belong to a religious institution like a church, a mosque, or a synagogue, maybe join one—you can also explore other religions that hold the same core values but are more forgiving when it comes to your lifestyle. Finding one of these open-minded religions isn't as difficult as you think. Most communities have a local ethical or humanist society, or Unitarian church—check it out on Google. Or find little religious traditions to bring to your household.

Pam, a stay-at-home mom in the Bronx, did just that when she first moved in with Russell, several years before they married. "Establishing our first home together—which I very much saw as the beginning of the rest of our lives together—inspired me to want to acknowledge the Jewish holidays and celebrations even more than I had done in the previous years living 'on my own' in college. I guess I wanted to lay down the foundation for family traditions to come."

What if the issue comes down to different religions? It's okay if you practice them separately, and as long as you can make them work together in the same home, you're fine. Heidi, a business manager in Oakland, California, says, "It was seriously the damn Christmas tree that made us realize we couldn't make living together work. I just didn't feel comfortable having one in my house, having grown up Jewish. And he didn't get it. Or,

TIPS FOR BEING SPIRITUAL WHILE LIVING IN SIN

Be sure living with him doesn't compromise your *personal* beliefs before moving in.

Know how your domestic situation impacts the personal values of both of you.

If you have questions, speak to a member of the clergy about how some religions view cohabitation, and make up your own mind accordingly.

Explore religions that condone cohabitation.

Find out ways to practice spirituality your own way, like attending religious services or making it a point to pray or meditate more often.

Bring traditions from your religion (or a religion you like) into your home and celebrate its holidays.

If your boyfriend practices a different religion, ask yourself whether you can find harmony between the two in your home. Find compromises.

Remember that as your relationship goes on, either of you could change your stance on religious practice. Talk about your beliefs and wants every so often.

Do your best to respect his religious beliefs. And be sure he respects yours.

probably it was more that he couldn't *not* have one in his house, having grown up Christian."

Deal-breakers could come up as you live together. It is always best to try to find compromises. However, within something as structured and emotional as religion and religious attachment, where do you go?

When Robin moved in with Chad, she says, "As far as our religious practices: they didn't change, I am Jewish and he is agnostic." But now they are discussing children, so "we have definitely had more discussions and are right now trying to figure out how to raise them."

Jessica, an administrative assistant from Winterville, North Carolina, says, "If someone believes in a higher power, that is their right. Just don't force it on me. He on the other hand has kept his Episcopal morals."

Ignoring an opposing religious belief is one way to go. But discussing it is a better bet. Keep the lines of communication open.

"I am Catholic and my guy is Zoroastrian," says Danielle, an occupational therapist in Dundas, Ontario. "We just respect each other's choices and beliefs."

Not Just a Number?

Sure, more of us are living together than ever before. But maybe because we're waiting longer to be sure we're ready for a long-term commitment. Check out these stats from the 2000 U.S. Census:

Median Age (in years) at First Marriage, from 1890 to 2000:					
YEAR	MEN	WOMEN	YEAR	MEN	WOMEN
1890	26.1	22.0	1950	22.8	20.3
1900	25.9	22.0	1960	22.8	20.3
1910	25.1	21.6	1970	23.2	20.8
1920	24.6	21.2	1980	24.7	22.0
1930	24.3	21.3	1990	26.1	23.9
1940	24.3	21.5	2000	26.8	25.1

Just like Romeo and Juliet?

So, what if your family and friends aren't opposed to cohabitation, per se, but they really just aren't supportive of your relationship? Well, Juliet, you need to handle the situation delicately, because, if Shakespeare taught us anything, it's that if you do ditch the fam for the sake of true love, the result ain't always pretty.

"There are two support systems that you need when you are in a relationship," says Lauree Ostrofsky, a life coach in New York

City who specializes in helping women make important life decisions. "First there is the support system you establish as a couple, with friends you choose together . . . and others who are supportive of you as a couple. Then there is that support system that belongs to you as an individual, made up of your family and friends. Both are really important to both of you individually and the relationship—and I mean they are of *equal* importance."

So, Mom and Dad don't like your wonderfully misunderstood guy? Even though it's tempting to avoid the issue—or just send the 'rents a text message saying you're moving in with Public Enemy Number One—it will inevitably do more harm than good.

"How you tell people you're moving in together has a lot to do with the history of that specific relationship," says Christy Calame. "In some cases it might be best to write a letter and never speak of it again. In other cases, you might suspect a person will see it as a greater betrayal if you tell them after the fact. Therefore, give them some time to process it before you move in. To some relatives who really value hearing it before it happens, telling them after you've moved in could add to their pain."

Truth is, your parents not liking your guy might not be such a difficult

HOW TO DEAL IF THE 'RENTS DON'T LIKE YOUR BOYFRIEND

Remember that their support is important to you, even though you really want to live with him.

Make sure you tell them you're moving in together in advance, even if you're afraid of their reaction.

Know that your parents are probably just being protective of you.

Listen to their perspective and take it into consideration, but make up your own mind about the situation.

Remind them that you're a responsible adult (assuming you are) and that you're making a well-thought-out decision.

Help them get to know your guy; they might end up liking him.

Ask a supportive family member to talk some sense into the others.

MOVING-IN MANTRA: ON MARRIAGE

"Marriage is a great institution, but I'm not ready for an institution yet."—Mae West

thing to work through. After all, it might just be a matter of them being protective of you. "My family told me not to move in with my boyfriend . . . In their eyes, no one was good enough for me, not even him," says Alicia, a financial advisor in Denver, Colorado. "We both had just graduated college, and we were going to do what we wanted to, despite what they said. After they knew it was happening, they helped me move in. From then on, they were always supportive and helped in whatever way possible."

So basically what we're saying is, your family might get over it once they realize you're an adult and can make your own decisions. "The goal is to be happy. No one wants someone else's negativity. And no one wants to be judged," says Calame.

One thing you could do is to help them all get to know each other. After all, when the two of you fight, they only hear their crying child on the phone chastising the bastard who won't put down the toilet seat. They don't know about the late night cuddlefest that made it all better. To facilitate a getting-to-know-him situation, utilize the family members who do support you. For example, if Dad doesn't like your boyfriend, but Mom

NICKNAMES YOU SHOULD NOT CALL HIS MOTHER
Mom-un-Law
Almost-Mom
Never-Mom
She-Who-Controls-Him
Miss Gulch (the alter ego of the Wicked Witch of the West)
Um, Wicked Witch of the West
Meddler
Crazy
Psycho
Hey you
. . . okay, you get it. Be nice.

sees the charm in that green mohawk, maybe she can give Pops a heads up that your honey's not such a bad dude. Just don't let things go too long before you ask her to have that talk.

Laura found out that her brother could have used a little getting-to-know-you time with her guy, but first a lot of time was wasted. "My brother wasn't supportive of my moving in with my boyfriend, since I had recently come out of a divorce," she says. "I didn't see my brother during the first year we lived together. Then, when we got married, my mom talked him into attending the wedding. To this day, my brother and my husband are good friends."

It shouldn't wait until a wedding, Ms. Procrastination. Get these talks started now!

Me Love You Long Time

Family and friends may also think you're rushing into your cohabitation situation, especially if you're young or you two haven't been dating long. Remind people that you can't put a timeline on love. Sometimes making it clear that you are moving toward marriage helps: "The fact that my boyfriend is a stand-up guy and not at all afraid of commitment—he's told them he wants to marry me—helps my parents handle our living situation better," says Sarah, a credit union manager in Columbus, Ohio.

Of course, if this isn't the case—if you don't want to get married or you aren't sure—you can try expressing that the two of you care about each other and will treat each other with respect and fairness while you live together.

The conditions of your living together can be another reason for your family to doubt you two.

"As accepting as my parents were of our relationship, they were uncomfortable with the idea of me being financially reliant on Russell," says Pam. "With the job I had at the time, it wasn't realistic for me to be able to pay an equal share of the rent and utilities. My parents loved and respected and trusted Russell, but because there was no ring on my finger, they were anxious about the dynamic of living in a household where he was in financial control."

When you put yourself in your family's and friends' shoes, you may realize that they're just worried about you, financially, emotionally or otherwise. Talking it out with them helps. And maybe they can help, too, to put everyone's mind at ease. Pam's parents gave her some money each month to help her pitch in for bills, so the contributions to the home were equal for her and Russell—and so that she could feel like an equal partner in their new home. "I realized that they were just looking out for my best interest," says Pam. "The arrangement came to an end after I got a promotion at work—slightly before we got engaged—and after enough happy months for everyone to feel even more comfortable with and confident in our relationship."

HOW TO ASSURE FAMILY AND FRIENDS THAT YOU'RE DOING THE RIGHT THING

Remind them that there is no timeline to follow when it comes to love.

Make it clear that you're serious about a future with this guy, if you are.

Make sure they know what a great guy he is; let them get to know him.

Express how much you two care about each other and respect one another.

Find compromises when it comes to any specific worries they have, like the financial situation.

Do what you can to make everyone feel comfortable and confident with the relationship.

Handling Sticky Questions

It's a thoroughly exciting experience when you decide to move in with your guy, but even in this day and age, there are some sticky situations that will arise, whether the people you love are open-minded enough to embrace cohabitation or not. And you can't let them squelch your excitement.

There are those people who remain mired in traditional or outdated notions. Here you are, setting up house and home with a man (a pretty cool one, in your eyes). Family and friends see you together, sharing toothpaste, loads of laundry and mac and cheese out of a box, vaguely resembling a married couple. "How serious are they?" they wonder. "What's going to happen next?" they ask. "They're so cute together, they should have a baby!" they think.

Brenda, a Web designer—and young, progressive, cohabitation-supporting woman—from Jersey City, New Jersey, once found herself saying, "Oh, I heard you got engaged. Congratulations!" to a couple that had just moved in together. When it became clear the two obviously weren't talking marriage yet, there was such an awkward silence that she wanted to crawl into a hole and hide, or at least to pause life like a bad Adam Sandler movie and think of some witty remark that would take it all back. "You'll probably encounter some dumb-ass like me," warns Brenda.

Sticky questions can be insulting, mean, or simply make you feel like someone is trying to impart their own values or priorities on to you. This is your relationship, not theirs—don't you know what's best in your own unique situation?

"Our parents have always been rushing us along," says Halle, a technology project leader in Los Angeles. "Sometimes we have to remind them that times have changed, that couples get married later in life and date much longer first."

You can't hold it against family and friends for asking you when you're going to get married or for trying to push you down that road, even if you're not sure you're going to go down it. It's difficult for people to change their long-time notions of what a family and a home are—and how they're supposed to be created. The best you can do is arm yourself with straight answers to tough questions.

First off, you should have some idea where the relationship is going, and should be in an agreement with your boyfriend on this one. It could be that you two agreed that you're just feeling things out, and that you're not aiming for marriage any time soon. Or it could be that you're thinking about marriage but you want to be sure you can live together first. Or it could be that you and your Romeo love being with each other so much, it just makes sense. Know the answer and stick to it! When they say "When are you going to get married?" something like "Well, Mom, I want to finish grad school before we discuss that" is a much better

WAYS TO HANDLE PEOPLE WHO PRESSURE YOU ABOUT GETTING MARRIED

Remind them that couples today date longer and get married later in life.

Don't hold it against them; they've probably had these notions for a very long time.

Arm yourself with answers to tough questions, like "Where is this relationship going?" To do this, be in agreement with your boyfriend.

Make sure their comments aren't making you confused about your own expectations.

Be honest and straightforward with them, and point out what's great about living together.

If they're annoying you or stressing you out in an extreme way, politely ask them to stop putting on the pressure.

Try to change the subject when you're uncomfortable.

Remember that if it's someone whose opinion isn't really important, you can just let it go.

response than getting mad and blurting the first thing that comes to mind (which might not be pretty). You might even be as blunt as Noa, a massage therapist from Scottsdale, Arizona: "I usually just say that we're living in sin and have no plans on changing it anytime soon."

"It isn't always that people are trying to suck, but it does feel a bit like a judgment," commented Caroline, a yoga instructor living in Edinburgh, Scotland.

Don't let those people's comments and questions make you lose sight of your own wants and expectations. Amanda found that a lot of her friends, who were getting married and having kids, were asking her when she and her boyfriend were going to get married. "Their comments would make me irate," says Amanda. "Marc and I were very happy to be moving at the pace we were. But unfortunately, their comments started to get into my head and cause me to start asking the same thing." Luckily, Amanda was able to eventually shake all that off. We like the honest, forward answer she used when people asked about marriage: "We are very happy where we are right now, love our life together, and don't need a ring to show our commitment to each other." Go ahead and steal it.

It's also okay to change what you want from your relationship as it goes on—and totally normal. Just be sure it's something that you want, not what someone else wants. And when you do start to change your mind, be sure to communicate that with your boyfriend as well. Be kind and patient because it might take some time for him to switch gears, too.

If the questions people are asking start to get to you, confuse you, upset or anger you, and if your clenched fists and teeth haven't stopped them coming, you *can* ask them to stop. Inform the offender that his or her repeated comments and/or questions are hurting your feelings and that you are quite finished defending the choices you are making in your life. Feel free to announce that for the time being you are not receiving advice and you are not fielding questions regarding your relationship but that you are, in fact, looking for some new pasta recipes. (Changing the subject is always a great way to move things along.)

Sometimes, when it's not worth a confrontation, you don't need to get into one. It's hard to change people's minds, so just let it go every once in a while. Like Sarah does sometimes: "Our darling, elderly neighbors—the wife is a pastor—think we're married, and I let them think it." If the person isn't that close to you, and their opinion really doesn't matter in the whole scheme of things, don't sweat it!

Or you could always wait till they ask, then point at the sky, shout "Look over there!" and turn and run.

Back Talk

Here are some of our favorite responses to tough—sometimes idiotic—questions:

"When my parents would ask when we were getting married, I would simply deflect and say, 'Ask *him*.'"—Robin

"There have been a few jokes, friends saying, 'Boy, didn't your parents waste a lot of Catholic school tuition on you!' I just stare those people down and don't break eye contact until they realize they're being idiots."—Jeanette

"I remind people that we are happy and committed to one another."
—Halle

"When a woman said, 'When is he going to make an honest woman out of you?' I told her, 'I'm honest now, was honest before I met him, and plan to stay honest.'"—Judith

finding and decorating your shared home

The first time I saw the place, it had faded purple shag carpets and a bathroom in the throes of a mildew meltdown. The blinking neon pizza sign outside the living room window didn't help my anxiety level. Neither did the overwhelming smell of garlic. Neal, on the other hand, was excited. He pointed out the hardwood floors underneath the putrid carpet and the potential for the twelve broken windows of the French doors. He insisted that a coat of paint would fix almost everything. A car backfiring outside may as well have been a gunshot. I hated it. But it was what we could afford. And all of a sudden I felt very, very poor.

—Heidi

Choosing your home together is an enormous decision. Where you live has a multitude of obviously significant ramifications on your life. Choose carefully and wisely. After all, this is the first of many compromises you'll make, so we'd chalk it up to good practice—if it wasn't so goddamn important. Few things are more essential to your happiness than the place where you rest your weary head at the end of the day.

We already went over buying versus renting. Now we're talking details: neighborhood, size, décor, features like a patio or balcony—maybe you're dying for a bathroom with a bidet. Of all those wonderful things that you want out of your home, the most essential, according to the women we talked to, was by far price. Most people aren't making their dream salary, but if you're both making about the same, then lucky you. You're both probably willing to shell out a similar amount each month.

Despite any disparity in your respective incomes, agreeing on financial decisions for your household is imperative before signing any dotted lines, proverbial or otherwise. If you make different salaries, find a compromise that you both feel good about. Tweak it later if necessary. But pay it close attention. As we've mentioned, money matters are sensitive and can make or break the peace.

"My boyfriend is the higher earner, so I didn't want to argue with him when he chose the place. I felt I didn't have much say in the matter," says Christine, a Montessori teacher in Toronto, Ontario. "It put a lot of stress on our relationship for a while because he knew that I wasn't happy. It defeated the whole purpose of my giving in."

Make sure you're both weighing in on the decision of where you live. Even if one of you has no income at all, it is important to remember that you are becoming a team. Trust us, getting steamrolled into living in Uzbekistan because you can't buy a vote won't be fun. Living together is a partnership, so a decision this important is best made together, no matter how much money is in the equation.

Another important factor in making a decision about where you will live is the amount of space you are able to get for your

MOVING-IN MANTRA: ON DECORATING STYLES

"I haven't taken my Christmas lights down. They look so nice on the pumpkin."—WINSTON SPEAR

money. We say get as much as you can. Seems pretty obvious. But when you consider splitting a $1,200 one-bedroom versus a $1,800 two-bedroom, it is easy to forget what exactly that extra $600 is paying for. In your saving-conscious haze, a one-bedroom apartment might seem okay, especially if both of you are used to living in small spaces. After all, how much room does one extra butt on the couch take up, right? Just remember that you will have twice the possessions you have now—maybe even more. "I couldn't believe how much stuff Thomas had to move into our place," says Jana, an anesthesiologist from Sewickley, Pennsylvania. "He had his gym, military, and sports gear. And I was shocked to discover that he had even more clothes and shoes than me. And guys' shoes take up so much more space in the closet!"

Trust us, a two-bedroom is worth the extra cash. Amanda agreed. "It was imperative that we have two bedrooms. We wanted to have extra space, just in case things didn't work out, or if we needed our own quiet time."

Amber says, "We chose the two-bedroom, even though it cost us more money. In retrospect, it was a good decision because it gave us a place to relax alone at times when we needed it. Plus it was a storage space for extra stuff."

What about the details? Hash things out before you even start apartment hunting. Does he require a gourmet kitchen? Do you need a place to park your moped? Be clear with each other about your expectations, but also be realistic. Know that unless money isn't an object, both of you won't get exactly what you want. Then, as you search for a place to call home, do little self-checks along the way to make sure you're still taking both perspectives into account.

In the end, one of your or his needs or wants may win out. "Commute time was the deciding factor," says Jeanette. "It's the D.C. area, the land of traffic and urban sprawl! Moving in with Stefan got me a thirty-minute commute. If he'd have moved into my place, it would have taken him over an hour to go twenty miles to get to work."

> **HOW TO CHOOSE A HOME WITH YOUR GUY**
>
> Compromise! The opinions of you both are important.
>
> Be sure you both agree on the price, even if you make different salaries.
>
> Space is huge. The huger the better. Spring for the extra bedroom if you can.
>
> Talk with him about the details you both want before you start looking. Be clear and realistic.
>
> Remember to take each other's desires into account as you look.
>
> Know that one of you may have to bend a little for the other to find a decision that works.

Yours, Mine, and Ours

His place has a great reading nook. Your place has an awesome washer and dryer. Where should you live? We vote: find a new place together. Make a fresh start. Think about it like this—you could break up your normal routine, pack up all your belongings and move into a place he's made his territory in every possible way short of peeing on the carpets. Or you could have him do the same for you. If you're set on moving into one of your already-occupied places, you're going to have to figure out—together—what is most important in making a compromise.

If it's a no-brainer—like you pay less in rent, but your place is huge, stunning, and close to both your job and his—make it work. First of all, get on the same page about what you expect when it comes to how things will change. Obviously the person living there will have to make room for the other's belongings, lifestyle, and taste in décor. Shelves will need to be cleared, drawers emptied, and impressionist paintings swapped with modern art (even though you think you could totally whip up something better yourself with macaroni and glue). If it is your place, get ready to rethink it as if you'd just moved in. If it's his, ask for the same courtesy. If you can, empty rooms of furniture to experience them from scratch. Give everything a massive cleaning—or, if possible, hire a one-time cleaning service to give you that brand-new feeling.

June says, "Aaron was not so keen on moving into my place even though it had the most space, the best backyard, and a dishwasher. So every time my roommate went away I made sure he spent time with me there to 'play house,' until he could start to see himself there and like it. And it worked: By the time my roommate was ready to move out, Aaron said that he was ready to move in."

TIPS FOR MOVING INTO HIS PLACE—OR HAVING HIM MOVE INTO YOURS
Know that things will have to change in the apartment.
Get on the same page about how it will change.
The stayer will have to make room for the mover's belongings, lifestyle, and taste.
Clear drawers and clean out half the closet in anticipation of the new person.
The stayer should rethink the apartment as if she/he just moved in.
Consider hiring someone to clean the place to make it feel new.
Be considerate! This will be a huge adjustment for both of you, no matter who's doing the moving.

Changes are inevitably tough for a lot of people. When you add a romantic roommate (AKA live-in boyfriend) to the mix, you can bet things get tricky. But the more prepared you are to meet tension head on, the smoother your lives together will be.

Duking It Out

Here are some ways to get your way when it comes to decorating (or most anything, really):

1. **Call it.** Like shotgun, if the car's in sight, the seat is yours. The same goes for rooms, drawers, and sides of the bed.
2. **Wrestle.** We'd like to teach the world to sing, but come on. It's so fun! Just have a code word so you know when to stop. You don't want to *really* hurt him.
3. **Debate it.** Women speak earlier in life and, some experts say, more eloquently than men. State plainly why the red vintage highback chair is just so much cooler than the nubby gray La-Z-Boy. Comfort should never get in the way of style!

Movin' on Up

Moving day. Those words are enough to strike fear in the heart of anyone who's been through it before, especially when there are two people involved. Especially two people with romantic passion and a sexual history between them.

"There is nothing funny about schlepping your belongings from two separate locations to one, using a U-Haul, while under time constraints," says Amanda.

Ultimately, we advise you not to strangle him. We also recommend that you do things in the easiest way possible to try to prevent the strangling urge. Wendy, a teacher in Manhattan, says, "Hire movers. Come on. Just choose sanity."

Trust us. It's worth it. Shop around for the best deal, and when you find it, let those guys or gals do the dirty work. If movers aren't an option, ask as many friends and family members as you can to help out. That worked wonders for Amber. "It took exactly forty minutes to move into our apartment," she says. Her strategy? "We had so much help and so little stuff. Twenty-five of the forty minutes were actually spent getting Neil's grandma's 150-pound, twenty-year-old sleeper sofa around the corner and into the apartment."

Having loved ones there will exponentially ease your pain. Concurs Cristina, a mental health counselor in New Port Richey, Florida, "Moving can be stressful, but our families were a big help." They'll act as buffers when you are stressed, so you're less likely to take it out on your boyfriend. They can also ease the pain of carrying that gigantic, heavy dresser up the stairs. Make sure you're mysteriously absent when that one gets unearthed from the truck. Just a tip.

If family and friends can't be there, at least be sure they'll be easily reached if you need some support. "Moving day was so difficult, not only because the place was a dive, but because it was so hot and muggy, and there was no phone to use to cry to my friends," says Christine. Maybe if she'd had someone to vent to—someone who wasn't her boyfriend—Christine could have gotten through it without having one of those breakdown moments when you find yourself thinking "What have I done?!" Have your cell phone handy and warn your friends and fam about the very real potential for a meltdown.

Also, give yourself plenty of man-hours—maybe even the span of a few days—and plan it for a nonstressful time in your schedule.

<table>
<tr><td>

MAKE MOVING DAY AS EASY AS YOU CAN

If you can afford them, hire movers—for everyone's sanity.

Ask family and friends to lend a hand.

If you can't get help, make sure a listening ear is only a phone call away.

Give yourself plenty of time to make the move—maybe a few days.

Try to be understanding of each other's moving styles.

Find the humor in all the craziness!

</td></tr>
</table>

Emily learned from her experience. "We had just returned to town from a wedding and we were leaving for two more that weekend in St. Louis and New York. We had one day to move in and we did it by ourselves with the help of my dad. We didn't finish until 2 A.M., and we'd started at 10 A.M. It was truly miserable." A little strategic planning, and you can avoid the move being more difficult than it should be.

Heidi says, "I got us a move-in date that overlapped with our current leases by fifteen days. If I hadn't been able to do that, I was prepared to go talk to the current tenants and see if they'd mind if we slowly began dropping things off. I figured I would have let someone else do the same. And it doesn't hurt to ask."

Also remember that you two may have two different moving styles. If you like things to be unpacked a certain way, know that he may have his own ideas. He might not like your methods either. "I had packed all my stuff in dozens of little boxes and purses, rather than in a few large boxes. My boyfriend found that incredibly frustrating," says Melissa. "I thought I was being smart, but it was tough to carry all those things."

Maybe you like everything neatly placed on and in the proper shelves and drawers right away, but he likes to slowly settle over a few days. Try not to let it get to you. Do your best to be as under-standing as you both were the day you told each other how many partners you've had. Of course, if it gets to be too much, move his still-packed-four-months-later boxes to the corner, cover them in a tablecloth and use them to display pictures and chachkas. He just might get the hint.

The best way of dealing with moving day is to make sure you both maintain your sense of humor. Make sure you can laugh about the little things.

"We opened up a box from his mom that had what seemed like 100 little crystal glasses, individually wrapped in this meticulous way. It looked so ridiculous, we took a picture, unwrapped each one, then played in the paper mess!" says Melissa. Now that sounds like fun!

Take It from a Pro

Here is some moving-in advice from Aleta Shaffer, an Emmy Award–nominated designer from *Queer Eye for the Straight Guy:*

1. **Purge!** Think of the stuff you get rid of as making room for new things. It is a necessary step when bringing his stuff into your life.
2. **Take measurements.** Know what will and won't fit. Use blue tape or masking tape to outline the size of the new sofa you are considering. That way, you can get a feel of how much space it takes up before spending the cash.
3. **Paint.** Match potential paint colors with items you are keeping. Then paint a square of that color on the wall and live with it for at least a week. Light changes all day long. It's important to see it in all of its phases.

4. **Economize.** If you see a great piece of furniture that is just too expensive, look on eBay and Craigslist. Eventually someone's going to be getting rid of the same one—for less than retail.

5. **Get organized.** There is no point in having something if you can't find it within five minutes. Seriously. You shouldn't even own it.

6. **Ask questions.** Utilize bookstores, libraries, and design blogs. On blogs, people are happy to offer great advice without making you feel like an idiot.

7. **Get creative.** Use cool wrapping paper as art. Frame a square to hang over a conspicuously bare wall. Or better yet, frame three. Another idea: Use a copier to blow up cool images from old books or even great landscapes you shot yourself.

8. **Don't be afraid of too much stuff.** You can always pare it down if it doesn't work. But you just might surprise yourself.

9. **Open up.** Make your two styles one whole new style. It is a magical concoction of one person learning to be whimsical and the other learning to be conservative—together.

How to Coordinate Black Rubber with Pink Chiffon

Teaching the Velvet Elvis you bought at Graceland on spring break in 2000 and your guy's grandmother's lace table runner, circa 1922, to live together in the same apartment or house is no easy task. There is your style and there is his style, and sometimes, even though you think the lace table runner is fine, even sort of pretty, it just isn't how you saw your dining room table. After all, what the hell *is* a table runner and where is it running? Right. So how do you keep that table runner from stepping on those blue suede shoes?

You knew that part of the challenge awaiting you when you agreed to live together was the compromises. In non-romantic roommate situations, everyone usually gets an autonomous bedroom and the living areas contain the functional minimum. As for decorating, it is often a democratic process, as in: "Yea to the oil painting of the grapes. Nay to the wagon wheel glass coffee table."

If there is a decisive "Nay" from anyone, in all fairness, the item generally needs to return to the autonomous bedroom of the owner of said offensive item.

Obviously, democracy is harder when there are only two of you and you are sharing every inch of space in the home. ("I hear one Yea and one Nay for the Cabbage Patch Doll collection. Tie. It stays!") The alternative? Negotiations. They will be inevitable and invaluable and will involve bargaining, begging, and copious amounts of guilt. When do you hold your ground and when do you make an effort to convince yourself that a Phish album cover could totally be the new Klimt?

Sometimes an item holds value. Whether it is a family heirloom or something otherwise economically or emotionally valuable, it is something important and should therefore be given longer and more thorough consideration.

Emily says, "I didn't like this yellow submarine cookie jar that his parents gave him. It's kind of growing on me, though. It's a Beatles collector's item."

Shaffer insists that sometimes that which is undeniably ugly can absolutely work. "In French it's called *jolie laide* and it means that something has off-key beauty. You can sometimes surprise yourself by making it a focal point or a conversation piece," she says. "Or you could always camouflage it."

TIPS FOR DECIDING WHAT STAYS AND WHAT GOES
Negotiate on what to keep and what to toss.
Bargain and make trades. Be fair about it.
Family heirlooms and potentially valuable items should definitely stay.
Try to see the beauty in the items he has that you don't like.
Know that you may have to get rid of some things he hates—and he might have to do some purging, too.
Live with *his* things that you hate because they mean keeping *your* things you love.

Still, you might find yourself having to say goodbye to the pink canopy bed your dad bought you for your sweet sixteen to make you feel like a princess. But don't worry, the trade-off is that your man might agree to get rid of his *Star Wars* pillowcases. (That is a resounding *might*!)

Sarah details her feelings on a choice item her boyfriend moved in with. "I hate his PlayStation," she says. "I wish a lightning bolt would selectively fry it."

Of course, you can always wish harm on those items you loathe. But in the end fairness and compromise are the best approach. Be considerate of each other. That's an obvious component of any relationship. But even though decorating should be fun, things could get ugly, and we're talking a fuchsia-toilet-cozy-made-out-of-yarn meets a baby-puke-green-tiled-bathroom ugly.

"I guess as long as I keep the dog," Sarah reasons, "he's keeping the PlayStation . . ."

How to Merge Your Stuff in Peace

So how do you begin? Once you are unpacking those boxes, it will all begin to unfold, or unravel.

There will be the rolled eyes, the audible sighs, and the less subtle "What the fuh . . . ?" As you go, you will sputter vitriolic laughter at the balls with which this man is approaching you with his white Ikea sofa with eight years' worth of TV dinner stains on every cushion. There is no way it is going to go anywhere within ten miles of a home in which you and your Dior curtains reside! He will likewise mumble under his breath, "but it's *purple* . . ." while staring uncomfortably at the trim around your desk. He won't care that it reminds you of your best friend's desk from the sixth grade that you coveted but never got to have until you were old enough to buy one yourself.

And you are off and running.

Our offhand advice is: Don't be rude to each other. If you say, "Really? You like this piece of shit?" figure he isn't going to reply, "Actually, I like all kinds of shit. From pieces to full logs. I just really love shit."

The fact is, he probably didn't think it was shit. So watch how you phrase it.

In some cases it won't be verbalized. It will be demonstrated.

"What he really, really dislikes is my fondness for throw pillows," says Amanda. "He would prefer to throw them around the bedroom rather than place them nicely on the bed."

Another strategy is to try not to take offense when he calls your Aunt Sylvia's old cuckoo clock the ugliest goddamn thing he's ever seen. Even though you both might try not to disrespect those items of his you don't want to live with and vice versa, inevitably you will.

Of course, if you really want it, we recommend that you start crying and explain that your Aunt Sylvia made you promise to care for that cuckoo clock after her lengthy battle with leukemia. That clock will hang front and center above the bed. Mark our words.

The Decorating Game

Don't worry. We ain't gonna market it to Milton Bradley . . .

1. Choose two rooms (or if you have just the one room, divide it into two sections).
2. Each of you draw up a plan for the design of one of the rooms. Use only the items you moved in with.
3. Switch, and draw up a design for the other room, again using only the items you arrived with.
4. Come up with an overall budget. Each of you propose an amount of money you are comfortable putting forth. (This can be based on factors from how much disposable income you have to how many items you need to make a comfortable home.)
5. Look at each other's designs.
6. Negotiate and update your designs accordingly. (In other words, if you forgot to include his cowhide rug, add it in. If you *purposely* forgot his cowhide rug, convince him that it would look better in his office or his brother's house.)
7. In the end, both of you will have completed two designs for each room. If the decision for which design is better isn't obvious, bring in a peanut gallery to vote. The winner for each room wins a free pass to keep an item that would have otherwise been voted off the island, er, out of the house. Or they win a back rub. After the big move, that may be an even better prize.

Muses

If you just can't agree on a style—or if, let's face it, between the two of you, you just don't have any—maybe what you need is a little inspiration. A trip to the library could be just the thing. Most libraries will have rows of books containing decorating tips of all kinds. You can also find back issues of design magazines for inspiration. Look at different eras like the crisp lines of Art Deco in the 1920s or the psychedelic colors of shag rugs in the 1970s. Explore styles from Old West to Mod. Rent movies from different eras and check out the furniture and the wall hangings. Look at the colors and the layouts. Shaffer recommends going for walks. "There are some incredibly inspirational shapes in nature," she says.

> **BEING POLITE ABOUT HATING EACH OTHER'S STUFF**
>
> Watch your phrasing. Try not to refer to things he owns as crap, shit, or dukie—in fact, just lay off the human-waste synonyms.
>
> Try not to be offended by his loathing. It's just stuff.
>
> Use guilt. He'll shut up quick.

Ultimately, decorating should be the fun part. It should bring you together like, er, folding together the sides of a sleeper sofa. Not rip you apart like, um, when your little brother got his hands on your Metallica poster at your eighth-grade slumber party!

We expound on the issue of space in Chapter 5, but if possible, make sure each of you has your own space where you can keep a few things that don't fit in the overall design scheme. It can be a drawer, a desk, a corner, or, if possible, a whole room.

What's Your Favorite Decorating Tip?

"Measure your curtains from ceiling to floor for long windows. The effect of the extra fabric on the floor will create a surprisingly elegant detail—I just learned that on the *Today Show*."—June, Brooklyn, New York

"I just want simple lines, not a lot of clutter everywhere, and cleanliness. Light colors, space and plenty of light."—Almudena, Burlington, Vermont

"I love decorating the mantle around the fireplace. I try to change it up every six or seven months."—Courtney, Columbus, Ohio

"Scoping the streets of New York for materials and furniture left on the street and upgrading them with help from plastic, glass, and metals stores."—Kerry, New York City

"Let each person in the household have a space that's totally theirs where they feel comfortable even if you think its ugly."—Callie, St. Paul, Minnesota

"We just add what we want and respect when the other one puts something that we don't love in the house, too."—Dianna, Baltimore, Maryland

Amanda says, "I let Marc do whatever he wants in his studio. He can keep it messy and tack things to the wall. His music equipment and records are stashed every which way. Whatever he wants goes. I avoid the space and when guests come, I close the door! This helps create balance between us."

Amber's solution, on the other hand, did not involve walls. She explains, "The style of our place was flea market. I don't think a single piece of furniture matched except for the pink floral couch and matching pink chairs from Neil's grandma."

Allow yourself to view your stuff as . . . well . . . stuff. Jeanette did just that. She says, "The most difficult part was finding a home for all my shit in this little townhouse. I had a three-bedroom apartment for years by myself and then went to sharing a two-bedroom townhouse." Her solution? "We made a deal before I moved out. I put garbage in trashcans at my apartment and Stefan would come over and take everything to the dumpster, so I wouldn't have to do it. It worked out really well."

> **GET INSPIRED TO DECORATE—AND DO IT!**
>
> Check out the decorating books and design magazines in the local library.
>
> Rent movies made in different eras and pay attention.
>
> Use nature as your muse.
>
> Create a design scheme and have fun with it.
>
> Have your own space where you can put things that don't fit the desired scheme.
>
> Make the most of what you have.

What to Do with the Mounted Moose Antlers

People's tastes can surely be a thing of wonder. Christine was forced by her guy to part with a flying pig she hung over their bed. "I think he thought it was funny, but it did not work for romance and sex." However, her unusual taste led her to admit that of the things he brought to their home, she really loved a toy tissue holder. "It makes different sounds when you press buttons and has not ceased to entertain me since I moved in with him." Still, not everything was that easy. So Christine made changes or modified items to suit her own taste—and lifestyle. "I learned to use all the stuff. For example, an antique table that is so not my style. I turned it into a liquor stand and it has been great for boozing!"

Jeanette managed to get her boyfriend to agree to something she couldn't live with. She explains simply, "He parted with the pet bird. We don't talk about it."

Meanwhile, Amanda achieved the impossible. She says, "He was a big fan of light wood, while I was in favor of dark. He has recently admitted to coming around to my side, though! I changed him. Ha!"

However, we don't expect everyone to achieve anything so impressive as the mythological "Changed Man." Seriously, don't even try. So here are a few tips for combining in harmony and making a home that belongs to you both. The easiest is to purge. Have a garage sale or sell things on eBay. All proceeds can go toward getting a few pieces you can share. (Can't sell it? Post it on a Web site like The Freecycle Network at *www.freecycle.org*. For free, *someone* will want it. You know what they say about one man's junk . . .) Also, try living with those things you find hideous—maybe you'll learn to like them or, better yet, convince him to hate them. The same goes for strangely shaped rooms, tight quarters, and bad lighting. Sometimes those things you thought would be the biggest challenges can turn into the best features about the place.

WHAT TO DO WITH THE STRANGE AND UNUSUAL

Admit that you also have weird things. He's not the only one.

Try to find a way to use it so it works with your life.

Give it time. Maybe he'll come around and agree with you.

Give it time (yes, we know we already said that). Maybe you'll learn to live with it.

Sell it at a garage sale or on eBay.

Can't sell it? Give it away.

Move things around to try to make it work better.

"Quirks have a way of surprising you," says Shaffer. "A funny corner might be the perfect spot for a day bed. A strategically placed bookshelf might end up creating a fantastic office space. Rearrange for inspiration. Don't be afraid to try something out."

moving to a new city—
his, yours, or new to both of you

We met while traveling in South America and fell madly in love. Then, after our trip, I went home to New York and he went to Kansas. We talked on the phone and visited each other a few times before we started saying, 'If we're going to make this work, we need to be in the same place.' He got here and I remember looking at him the moment he arrived and the only thing I thought was—to my own surprise— 'this was a huge mistake.' I mean, didn't I spend the last five months talking to him every night on the phone and whispering about how excited I was for him to arrive? And then he arrived and bam! it was real. He moved in with me with the plan that it would be until he found his own place. He was stressed out looking for a job and trying to get comfortable in a new place—totally understandable!—but the result was he didn't pay me much attention, was not very loving, was often stressed, frustrated, and annoyed and was quite selfish. We didn't have a lot of sex. He wasn't generous with money. I paid rent—he never offered to help. When I brought up my concerns and sadness, he was very unreceptive.

—Louise, journalist, New York City

The world seems just a bit smaller than it used to, right? You can hop a flight and vacation in Paris for the summer, St. Martin for the winter (or, job depending, a week in either one). You can call anywhere in the United States with your free long distance. At any moment your job could move you to the Chicago branch or, if you live in Chicago, to the branch in L.A. Not to mention the fact that you can chat online with guys from any country in the world—or even one just in the next county.

With job transferring, finding romance online, or being away at school, there's bound to be some talk of moving—for you, him, or the two of you together. So how do you decide who moves where? Move to his town? Have him move to your town? Or move somewhere new to both of you?

"You need to do a lot of talking before making this decision. You want to make sure that you both see the future the same way," says Fiona, a doctoral candidate in Pittsburgh, Pennsylvania.

Is the move temporary or permanent? What is the potential for his and your careers in the new place? How serious is the relationship, and what will having moved mean if you're not together forever?

"I told him that I didn't need to be engaged to move, but that I needed to know that he could picture marrying me," says Fiona.

"Make sure you're prepared for how things would be if it didn't work out," warns Kerry, a publicist in New York City.

If one of you is used to moving around a lot, has a job you hate, or is running from the law, it should be pretty obvious who's in a better position to move.

"We wanted to live together, but weren't quick to decide which city one of us would move to at first. We put it off, even though at three months we knew we wanted to be together," says Kerry, who used to live in a different city than her boyfriend. "Finally, I was being laid off due to a corporate take-over and I didn't have family where I was living. The decision was made for us."

If it's not such an easy decision, weigh all the big personal factors: How important is living near friends and family to each of you, and how far away from them will you be? How important are your careers to each of you—will you be happy with your job and salary in the new place?

Here's how Fiona and her guy hashed it out: "First of all, he lived in Pittsburgh, and I lived in Connecticut which had a high cost of living. We decided we weren't interested in pay-ing $600,000 for a fixer-upper! Sec-ond, jobs went into the decision. At the time, our jobs were about equal in terms of pay, but his job had more future opportunity. Third, his family lived in Pittsburgh while I had no one close in the area I was living."

For Courtney, who works in pro-motions in Columbus, Ohio, friends were a factor, too. "Brian knew I had

QUESTIONS TO DEBATE WHEN DECIDING WHO SHOULD MOVE
Is the move temporary or permanent?
What is the potential for both your and his careers?
How serious is the relationship, and what will having moved mean if you're not together forever?
Is moving easier for either one of you for any reason?
How important is being near friends and family to each of you, and how far away from them will you be?
How important are your careers to the two of you? Will you be happy with your and his job and salary in the new place?
Who has the more desirable home, and how easy is it to sell your homes or get out of your leases?
What is the culture, cost of liv-ing, and climate of the towns the two of you are considering, and how would those affect your lifestyles?
Would you both move for the other if necessary? Why or why not? What does that say about your relationship?

lived here my whole life and had developed lasting friendships. While we dated, he got to know many of my 'couple' friends and really grew to like them and develop his own friendships here in Columbus," says Courtney. "I also had the bigger house and the bigger yard for his dog . . . I would have moved for Brian, but I was extremely happy I didn't have to!"

Remember that moving to a new city is expensive. The person moving will probably end up with time off work and a pricey bill from the moving company.

Also, consider the culture of the new town. If you're a big-city girl, used to sending out your laundry and ordering sushi take-out, moving to the country might not provide the lifestyle you're used to. Even climate and cuisine could come into play, if outdoor activities and being a foodie are really important to you. Try to think of it all while you're hashing it out.

This decision should be important to both of you—we'll get into more about how the move affects both the mover and the stayer as this chapter goes on. At first make sure you're both in agreement and that this is what you both ultimately want. If both of you *would* move for the other, but one plan is smarter, for whatever reason, then that's a sign you're making the right decision.

The Mover and the Stayer

Okay, so moving to a new town can be hard—and moving in with someone can be complicated. (We mean, seriously, we wrote a whole book about it.) So how can you help each other through this time? First of all, remember that a move can be pricey. If one of you doesn't have a job in the new place yet, has sacrificed a security deposit, or is otherwise being financially challenged by the move, it might be appropriate for the stayer to help out with paying the movers as well as other moving costs as they come up. Or if the stayer is unable to help the mover out financially, maybe he or she could invite some friends over and ask them to pitch in on moving day. For some odd reason, most friends will happily lift heavy furniture as long as there is the lingering promise of two things that can be purchased on every street corner in America—there's just something about pizza and beer and moving! But even if the mover—say, your guy—is just bringing a few boxes full of things, we think the stayer—say, you—should do something. After all, this is your chance to make a new first impression on the person you love. Don't eff it up. Carry the damn books.

HELP EACH OTHER THROUGH THE MOVE
Volunteer to help with moving expenses.
Call friends to help with the physical labor.
Pitch in.
Offer emotional support.
Listen to each other.
Do what you can to make each other feel comfortable with the change.

Or at least buy the pizza that gets someone else to carry them!

As far as emotional support, be sure you're giving that to each other, too. The mover might be homesick, lonely, lost, or overwhelmed in the new place. The stayer might also feel overwhelmed, as well as invaded. They might be mourning their independence. Be sensitive to these matters. Listen to each other when you're expressing your feelings. Make sure you're *really* listening and try to make each other feel comfortable accordingly.

City Swap

There are three moving-to-another-city scenarios that you might find yourself in, and here's what to think about depending on which one you find yourself in.

Scenario #1: You Move to His City

Just because you're moving to his city doesn't mean you need to move straight into his house. Of course you have to decide whether you're ready for cohabitation, just like any other girl moving in with her guy. Maybe you should start off in separate homes, at least for a trial run. After all, moving in with him will mean two new, huge adjustments, as opposed to one. You're invading *his* space, *his* apartment, *his* town, *his* life. And you're giving up *yours*.

"I was afraid of losing my independence," says Gracie, a program manager in Burlington, Vermont. "I had always thrived on the fact that I had friends and activities that were mine, like meeting friends after work for a drink, yoga classes, running in the park, etc. I was also sad about losing the investment I'd made in figuring out my favorite places to eat, wander, get coffee or window shop. I was really worried that I wasn't going to find easy replacements for those simple pleasures."

"I moved from Los Angeles to Detroit [to be with him]. I was afraid I was going to hate it and be bored," says Kerry. "I really got caught up on the things my friends were doing every night in L.A., and I was sad I was missing out. It wasn't that I didn't want to be with Mark, I wanted to do those cool things *with* him."

Know that it will take a lot of work to get a life in his town, to make it your own. First, find a job as early as humanly possible.

"I got a job before I moved there," says Fiona. "I would highly recommend this strategy even if it takes longer. Getting a job can take months! Also, if you're not employed yet . . . it will be harder to develop your own life and could put stress on the relationship. It was definitely good to have a job where I could go every day and could meet new people."

If you're initially unhappy in the new place, it's important to deal with it in a healthy way. Kerry regrets her overemphasis on work in the new town. "I found a job with a professional sports team. That became my life. I worked weekends, nights, and holidays. Whenever we played a game at home, basically," says Kerry. "It's not the ideal life for someone who doesn't *love* what they do."

Instead, find social activities, exercise, spend time outdoors, make new friends. Basically get off your lazy ass and do things that make you happy!

Of course, you've made a sacrifice for him, but that doesn't mean you shouldn't be making yourself happy, too. "I struggled with balancing the

---

STRATEGIES FOR WINNING OVER HIS FRIENDS AND FAMILY

Show them you can be "one of the guys." Tag along for football and wings night. Order a giant, imported beer and a plate full of wings.

Let him continue with any rituals established before you got there. If there is a night a week he and his boys play poker, don't take it away from him.

Ask his female friends if they want to go out for pedicures or to catch a chic flick, or maybe start a poker game of your own!

Be open-minded about his female friends. Try not to be catty or competitive.

Invite his friends with girlfriends/boyfriends out for double dates.

Offer to bring something along to his friends' house party. If they say no, bring a bottle of wine anyway. When you get there, offer to help prepare food or pour drinks.

Don't just make small talk—ask them lots of questions about themselves.

With his family, do the same things we listed above: make an effort to fit in, show you want a relationship with them, invite them to do things with you two—or just you—and offer to help out. You'll be the best girlfriend he's ever had.

fact that this decision was a step toward strengthening our relationship and wanting to focus on our togetherness, while knowing in the back of my mind that we should also be nurturing our selves," says Gracie.

Remember: even though you're far away from your family and friends, that doesn't mean you can't go to them for support.

"I swallowed my pride and reached out to old friends and my sister. Those ladies were amazing. Even from far away they reminded me why I'd made this choice, talked me out of feeling hopeless, and pushed me to connect with the ways I'd found fulfillment before," says Gracie. "They also rallied to visit, which forced me to look for fun things to do. Every time they mentioned things they liked about my new home I started to see the good things that were here instead of just missing what I'd left behind."

Remember that you can lean on him a bit, too. Ask him to take you on a tour of the city and point out landmarks and his favorite places. Go with him to the restaurants and bars he likes. Or embark on a mission to create new "regular hangouts" together. Meet his friends, family, and coworkers, and win them over with your sparkling personality. You may find that his friends become yours and that his family is actually kinda cool to hang out with.

"In the new town, I got to spend more time with his family, with whom he is really close. It gave me a better understanding of who he is as a person and where he comes from," says Kerry. "It was difficult at first for me since I'm not too much for family, but ultimately, it was a good experience for me to get used to the idea of having family around."

Make sure you also spend time carving out your own niche. Remember that you could put a lot of pressure on the relationship if you make it your sole priority. Take a class or join a club. Invite coworkers to lunch or out for drinks. Don't forget to maintain ties to your friends back where you came from. Make it a point to try out new restaurants, bars, boutiques, bakeries, and theaters—maybe take him to one he's never been to. Buy tickets to sporting events and concerts, or attend exhibits of artwork by local talent. Anything to help you feel more a part of the community!

Even just go to the park and hang out. You may be surprised by how friendly people can be and how welcome they might make you feel.

So, not only are you adjusting to his new city, but you're adjusting to moving into a new apartment. Should you move into his place or find a new one together? You'll obviously need to do what's right for the two of you, but we'll give you the same advice we gave people who began their cohabitation in the same city: look for a new place together.

"We found a new place for us to move in to together," says Kerry. "I would totally recommend this because then everything was new and everything was *us*. I didn't feel like a visitor. It was actually the first time I felt at home at my place because with roommates I never felt like it was *my* home.

THINGS TO REMEMBER WHEN MOVING TO HIS TOWN

Make sure you're ready to move in together. If you're having your doubts, consider starting off in your own place and move in with him after you've had some time to settle.

Finding a job before you move is a smart decision and can help you avoid a potential strain on your relationship.

It will be an adjustment and you may feel homesick—that's perfectly normal at first! Handle it in a healthy, constructive way.

Get to know the city through him and for yourself.

Make friends through him and for yourself.

Your friends and family may be far away, but you should still keep in regular contact with them.

Spending time with his family—if they're nearby—may make you feel more at home.

Moving in with Mark, I felt like it was *my* place with him. He's the best roommate I've ever had."

Determined to move into the place he already lives in? You've got to find a way to make *his* place *yours*, too—without totally freaking him out. Before you get there, map out a plan as far as what furniture you'll be moving in—he may have to move some things around. Then, warn him that you will want to make a few changes to the place to make yourself feel more at home (see Chapter 3 for tips on merging your belongings and making it look good).

When you get there, don't try to take over the whole house or the everyday routine—but also don't sit back and leave everything as you found it—politely explain that now that you're a part of his life there, he'll have to make some changes, too. If he eats pizza every night in front of the TV, it may take a while to convince him that you should cook healthy meals together and dine at the table. Express what's important to you for feeling at home. Compromise accordingly. Maybe you both agree to have TV dinners three days a week, cook three days a week and eat out one. Just because he's done it one way in this place by himself for all this time, doesn't mean he shouldn't change things up for you when you're there, too.

And, we must reiterate, make sure he puts you on the lease and you split up the bills. "I moved into the apartment that he was already living in, so my name wasn't on lease or any of the

TIPS FOR MOVING INTO HIS PLACE
Map out a plan for your belongings before you load the moving truck.
Discuss inevitable changes.
Compromise when it comes to your daily routines and particulars.
Put your name on the lease and split up the bills.

bills," says Fiona. "So when I tried to get my Pennsylvania driver's license, I didn't have enough 'proof of residency.'"

Scenario #2: He Moves to Your City

Feeling lucky that he's moving to your town? Before you start thinking you have it so easy, know that you'll make it much easier on him—and on you—if you help him out.

You know how we said in the last section that finding a new job before you move to a new city will make things vastly easier on the relationship? Well, duh: maybe you should help him find a job. Remember that you have contacts in your town—he may not.

"I have a friend whose husband is a partner in a landscape architecture firm, and she was able to get Brian an interview. He was quickly hired for a great job with MSI Design," says Courtney.

Ask your uncle, cousins, friends, that neighbor down the hall who owes you a favor for walking her dog while she was away—whoever might help. You never know who someone knows. If you don't have good connections in his field, maybe it's just a matter of searching the newspapers or Web sites for postings and passing them along to him, or maybe you can help him proofread or design his resume, if that's a talent you have.

When he gets into town, help him learn his way around. Take him to the coolest places—the spots that will make him fall in love with your city. Do things that are up his alley, like checking out local sporting events or venues that feature the kind of music he likes.

Make him feel welcome in your apartment, if he's moving straight in. Put him on the lease—you may have to pay a small fee, but it will be worth it for both of you to know that you're equal partners with equal responsibility. Clear out drawers and cupboards just for him, or move out excess furniture to make room for his stuff. He hates your TV? Go shopping together and find one you both agree on. He's bound to notice your effort and it will make him happier and less stressed.

Remember that the changes that come along with him moving in may seem difficult to deal with at first, but they might actually prove to be for the better.

"I've never had a dog before, so I was nervous about the dog moving in," says Courtney. "Not that I didn't love Boo—he is the greatest dog ever! But I'm kind of a neat freak around the house and Boo is a shedder. The thought of hair everywhere made me hesitant. At first, there were rules: The dog can't be near the couch; the dog can't come in our bedroom; all the doors need to stay shut. It took about two or three months, but now there are no rules. In fact, we got a second dog and they pretty much run the house. I love them to death—hair and all!"

Let in new ideas and new things. Remember that you will have to change some routines, like suddenly you may have to rock/paper/scissors for Wednesday night TV if your favorite shows compete. Now you will have to consider renting movies *he* wants to watch, tagging along with him to his work events, and generally making him a part of a life you've already established.

"Since we had met abroad, he didn't know my family and friends," says Cecile, a landscape architect in New York City. "My biggest worries were not between the two of us, but how he would transition into my world."

Help him out by creating comfortable environments in which he can meet your friends and family. Throw a housewarming party for him so that he has the opportunity to gravitate naturally to friends of yours with whom he might have more in common.

Use your best judgment to figure out which of your friends he might hit it off with and make plans with them, especially couple friends and groups. It might take some time for him to feel completely comfortable, so be patient. Don't expect him to suddenly decide on his own to call your guy pals up to watch Monday night football. But maybe the guys are all going out golfing, and you can suggest *they* invite him along. (You might not want to let him know it was your idea, though.)

"I encourage him to go out with my best friend's husband. They have a lot of similar interests, and they have been to concerts and sporting events together. They also enjoy a night of Guitar Hero whenever they can squeeze it in," says Courtney.

You may even facilitate some other social opportunities for him, too, if the situation is right. Courtney also took some initiative to help develop her boyfriend's social life. "Brian's friend from Lima recently moved to Columbus. I got him hired with my company. I think Brian likes living near his old friend as well.

TIPS FOR DEALING WITH HIM MOVING TO YOUR TOWN
Help him out with things like finding a job and learning his way around.
Show him the best places in town to help him love the city as much as you do.
Take him to do things that are right up his alley.
Make him feel welcome in your apartment by clearing out room for him and going shopping together.
Remember that change in your home can be good. Let new ideas into your routine.
Let him get to know your family and friends. Encourage his relationship with them.
Never let him come between you and your family and friends.
Do all that helping, but let him do some work on his own, too. Independence is important for both of you.
Remember to keep your independence, while showing him that your relationship is a priority.

"I really wanted Brian to make some friends of his own in Columbus," she continues. "One thing he really missed was his poker nights in Cincinnati. He keeps talking about starting up a poker night in Columbus, but it hasn't happened yet. I keep encouraging him to do that."

Don't worry. Eventually he will make his own friends as well. You might have to be patient, but it will happen. The best thing you can do in the beginning is to be encouraging—and give him the time and space to do that. So go ahead and maintain some of your old routines without him, too. Keeping an ongoing "girls' night" is the ultimate way to do that.

There are other things he's going to have to do on his own, too. Find his way around, schmooze at work, get involved in his own clubs and activities. Feel free to encourage him, but, ultimately, leave him some space. He's a dude—he's not gonna like keeping to some rigid social schedule you create. Think of it as a fifty-fifty ratio: you help him out with about 50 percent of the adjustments he needs to make. Or gauge it by his personality. A really outgoing guy used to moving around a lot may need more like 10 percent help. A guy who's lived in the same town all his life and is acutely shy might need 75 percent.

You may need to adjust your own schedule to account for his lifestyle. But remember that you shouldn't completely overhaul it. Be sure you're still making time for your family and friends, yet also showing him that your relationship is a priority, too. After all, they're both really important. (More on that later.) Again, *you* didn't move. You do not need to behave as if you did. It'd be like men who have sympathy cravings when their ladies are pregnant. We think that's weird, too.

Scenario #3: Moving to a New City Together

You're graduating college together and looking to grow roots somewhere else. Or one of you is having a job transfer or starting a graduate program in another town. Maybe both of you are just sick and tired of living where you do so you're picking up and moving.

"We met in Santa Cruz. I went to UCSC and he went to Berkeley. We moved to New York together since he works in film and I work in magazines and it's basically New York City or L.A. [for those industries], and we wanted to get out of California," says Lindsey.

So you're in a new place. If you don't know anyone there, you will have to deal with the fact that you're each other's only friends, maybe even only "family."

"I think there were many benefits of moving to a new place the first time we moved in together because we were away from the pressure of family and friends," says Amber. "Ultimately, we missed their support and chose to move back, but I think it was a good thing initially so that we had to lean on each other more and couldn't escape easily from obstacles by always turning to others. It has also helped our relationship because we learned how to be our own family and put each other first."

Of course, you will need your own friends some of the time— so, as we've established, it's important that you find them once you're there.

"We made friends individually and together," says Amber. "Neil started coaching hockey and we met a nice couple that way, too. We each had work friends. We also had a mutual college friend who later moved to the area."

Seriously, get a life with him and without him. It will make your lives feel fuller—not to mention fun! "We loved spending time together and yet I had a life, he had a life, and we had a life—a distinct separation was never necessary because there was always an innate understanding of independence and commitment," says Cecile. That's the goal!

Often, moving to a new place with your guy means hard times ahead. You could have to adjust to a whole new culture. There may even be a language barrier. Maybe you're just starting out together, or one of you is supporting the other through school—or you're just moving to a place with a really high cost of living.

Take it from Amber who was in medical school. Her guy was supporting them both financially in the new city, where he moved for her.

"It was hard because we didn't have much money and had to live in an area that wasn't ideal for his career path, so that made finding and keeping a job hard. He worked really hard and did whatever job he could find until a decent one came along. I remember when he was laid off from his first job after we moved there. He was so disappointed because he really wanted to support me. We worked together to find a better one, and in the meantime he worked as a waiter and sales clerk even though he didn't like it. I really admire him for that, and it definitely made us stronger that we went through that time, when things were far from perfect, as a team."

TIPS FOR MOVING TO A NEW TOWN TOGETHER
Be friends and "family" to each other. Be supportive of each other.
Make friends together and separately by getting involved in your own groups.
Be sure you're balancing independence and supportiveness.
Get through hard times as a team and find the romance in it.

Cecile has a similar story: "At that time, we were short on money and would spend hours each night playing chess on a hand-made board with pieces made from the local hardware store in our tiny room saving up for our own place away from roommates."

Yes, it could be a struggle. There could be obstacles when it comes to moving to a new place. But luckily, you have each other to get through it.

"It was much easier with two people," says Lindsey. "It would have been rough on my own."

Remember that you are doing this together for a reason; keep that perspective in mind.

"We worked through that time together, and honestly, we had a strong desire just to be together and this is what we had to do in order to do that," says Amber. "It's funny how hard times are often the most romantic times as well."

Seriously, what's more romantic than not being able to pay the electric bill and having to spend a whole week burning candles and groping around in the dark (or just groping each other)?

5.

boundaries, respect, and privacy

I'm an only child, and I don't like people touching my stuff or being around me all the time—gee, I sound lovely! From the beginning, I told Jon not to touch my stuff, which he thought was weird, but he went along with it. When we'd lived together for a month or so, I told him that I needed some 'quiet time,' that I'd be in the bedroom with the headphones on full blast for a couple of hours, and not to bug me unless there was a fire. I still do that sometimes—I don't always use the headphones; I can just tell him it's quiet time and go to another room. If I'm especially bitchy to him, even now, he'll ask me first if I'm hungry and second if I need my 'quiet time.' He doesn't worry about that stuff at all. He could care less if I use something that's his, as long as I don't mess it up, and he doesn't need space that's just for him. I'm more difficult, so I'll tell him 'that's mine—don't mess with it!'

—Jen

Space. The final frontier? Maybe. Once you're living with your guy, it can be a hot commodity. Here you are: Two people. One home. Lots of togetherness. Chances are you get moony thinking about how sweet all that time together will be.

But the thing is, when you live apart, everything you do together—from watching reruns to updating your résumés—is, in essence, a date. But living together finds you spending every at-home moment with each other. Some of these moments, like when you're cooking Thai food, are fun. Others, like enduring the stomach flu, are, well, like enduring the stomach flu. If you work it just right, pairing the good with the bad can make your relationship stronger.

To do this, you might end up setting some boundaries—both physical and emotional—that will give you and your relationship the breathing room necessary to facilitate a wild and frenzied growth spurt. While a certain amount of growing together is inevitable and encouraged, no one recommends that the two of you end up in a vise grip. Unless, of course, at least one of you is naked . . . But that's a totally different chapter.

Get a Room!

We're guessing you aren't fortunate enough to have your own wing. (I'll take West, you can have North. East and South are common ground.) You might not even have more than one room. But you should definitely have your own space—a desk, a bureau, a chair, a corner, a whole room if you're lucky. Ideally, it's a place where you can go when you need some alone time or to work on the reports you occasionally have to bring home. It might just be some place you can keep your jewelry without it getting mixed in with his aftershave. This, of course, depends on your own, personal desire for space—and how much there is to spare.

"In our office, we designated half of it for Neil and half of it for me," says Amber. "We each have our own desk and shelves. Ideally we would each have our own office but since we don't, we have to respect each other's space by not touching the other person's things. It keeps things harmonious. Well, it keeps me harmonious. I need to know that if I keep pens in the top left drawer, that's where they will be the next time I go rifling for one. If that's all the space I get, I really come to rely on that."

PIECES OF THE HOME TO DESIGNATE AS YOUR OWN

A desk, a bureau, a chair, or other piece of furniture

A corner

A whole room

Half a room

A separate bathroom

If the size of your home is such that you are down to designating corners and pieces of furniture to call your own, it can be easier if it is something you brought from your old place, like your grandmother's rocking chair. It can also be something you buy for this express purpose: a desk, an armoire, a very very large box. Just knowing that there is a place to call your very own—in a space where you're surrounded by him, him, and more him (if you haven't felt this way yet, be prepared)—will help you stay sane.

"For me and Jonathan, separate bathrooms were key," says Alex, a teacher in Memphis, Tennessee. "He wasn't used to having ten million beauty products hanging around, and I got that."

Respect

Both of you should consider these strategies for putting each other's boundaries first.

R—Room. The more room the better. If you haven't moved in together, consider getting a slightly bigger place to be sure you can each have a bit of your own space, in addition to all that you'll share, of course.

E—Equality. Women tend to ask for alone time. He might not, but he needs it, too. Give him the same consideration he gives you when you've had a bad day.

S—Sense of humor. Don't take every invasion of space so seriously. So he accidentally walked in on you clipping your toenails, when you told him you needed a few minutes. Make a joke and move on!

P—Perspective. Take his into consideration, especially if your opinions differ when it comes to how many (and what kind of) boundaries there should be. Everyone has different wants and needs, and you should be sympathetic to his.

E—Exceptions. Make them! Maybe you've asked him not to bug you while you're doing your favorite kickboxing DVD—even if it's to give you a little kiss. That's your right. But every once in a blue moon, make it a point to pause the DVD, find him, and lay a smooch on him.

C—Communication. If you're not getting the space you need, let him know in a calm, rational way. Watch the passive-aggressive behavior! It will only make things worse.

T—Tact. He might be totally embarrassed by something he used to formerly do in private. (Stink up the bathroom, for example.

Eeew!) If it bothers you that he doesn't light a match (or use air freshener, or turn on the fan—whatever floats your boat), be kind when you bring it up.

Sharing, Caring, and Scaring

We're not calling you a control freak or anything. But we're sure there are plenty of things you like to have a certain way—so in the past, you've kept them to yourself. Pointing out what is private and what isn't from the beginning will help thwart that moment he mistakes your journal for your great-grandma's book of recipes.

Inevitably, whether you like it at first or not, there is likely to be a whole host of shared items. But if you are sharing a desk or a dresser due to limited space, at least try to split up the drawers or shelves. It probably goes without saying—but thought we should still say it—that he might want his own plot of square footage, too. It's only fair.

Sometimes it's hard to bring up who gets what and what goes where but neither one of you wants to end up strong-armed into accepting, for example, dirty razors in the drawer where the toothbrushes live.

Meanwhile, we women are in constant struggle with vanity. Whether it's waxing, plucking, dyeing, drying, or shaving, a lot of products and hardware get us to our best manicures and our most perfectly coifed bangs. Some of these appliances should probably never be approached without steel-toed shoes and power tools. Hell, some of them *are* power tools. And they have to go somewhere. But where?

"In the bedroom, bathroom, and office we sort of have our own sides. It's more or less down the middle except that I have more stuff so my things probably bleed into his areas," says Amy, an editorial assistant in Hoboken, New Jersey. Dividing your storage space from his may keep you both sane—try to do this from the beginning.

Realize that "bleeding" (as Amy puts it)—or overlapping—is okay if you two know how to share, but it's not always as easy as it sounds. Gradually work it into your life. "It was weird to all of a sudden have to share in my house," says Courtney. "After my boyfriend moved in, I remember one of the weirdest things was having to put up pictures of *his* family and friends in what had been *my* house for the past four years. In the past all the pictures there had been mine, and now all of a sudden a different family is on the mantle. In the past few months, I've grown to really like that, and it makes me feel even more at home to see his family around our house as well." Know that you'll have to share, but voice your opinion if something feels truly uncomfortable. You'll probably learn to compromise over time. Remember that sharing stuff can almost be symbolic of you two sharing your life together—the more open you are to sharing, the more it permeates your entire relationship.

WHAT TO REMEMBER WHEN DESIGNATING WHICH SPACE IS WHOSE

From the beginning, point out what you *know* you want to stay private.

If something, like a dresser or closet, is shared, split up the shelves or halves.

Keep in mind that he should get plenty of space, too.

Take sides in the bedroom and bathroom, but know that there will inevitably be some overlapping.

Gradually learn to share.

If space merger feels uncomfortable, let him know.

Be willing to compromise.

Taking It Personally

Whether you're big on physical space or not, you'll need some *personal* space, for sure. Remember that alone time you could have whenever you wanted before you moved in together? Sometimes it's hard to break it to someone who loves being with you that you need to be away from him for a little while. But hold your ground. It is a request that is both completely normal and maybe even imperative to the health and well-being of you both—individually and together. Just be nice! If you're afraid to offend him, give him a good reason for the alone time.

Leigh, a dentist in Detroit, Michigan, explains, "I usually tell my boyfriend I need to take a bath when I want to be alone after a bad day. He completely lets me go, and I have an hour to me. I can unwind, cry, listen to music—really, do whatever I want."

Yes, it's *okay* to need some time by yourself, even if it's for no reason at all. "Some people meditate for alone time," says relationship expert, Christy Calame. "If you are together all the time, burnout is probably inevitable." In fact, some experts say that the mentally healthiest people quietly think, pray, or even do nothing, with no distractions, for at least fifteen minutes a day. And even though you're crazy about him, he does count as a distraction.

The Cuddling Controversy:
5 Ways to Convince Him You Should Cuddle Tonight

1. Once you're in bed, put the cuddling moves on him. Be smooth. Yawn and put your arm around him.
2. Roll over him and hold him down with all your weight. He's not getting out.

3. Whine for a while. Maybe make puppy dog eyes at him and push out your lower lip.

4. Give him a little back rub, or run your fingers over his back. Once you've lulled him to sleep, he is at your cuddling mercy.

5. Um, hello? Have sex with him. After his world is rocked, he won't be in any state to argue.

5 Ways to Convince Him It's Not *the Night to Cuddle*

1. Sigh repeatedly, saying that you're so tired. Roll away from him in bed and hope for the best.

2. If he tries to spoon, keep coughing and clearing your throat. (What? You have a cold!) He won't want to be so close to the commotion.

3. "Accidentally" touch your cold feet to him as he hugs you— ooops, you're sorry that you shocked him. In mental hospitals they say shock therapy can work wonders!

4. Okay, you can be nice and simply explain that you have to get up early in the morning, and it's hard to fall asleep mid-snuggle.

5. Hmmm . . . Have sex with him and then avoid him for the nine seconds it takes him to start snoring.

It Ain't Weird if Everybody's Doing it

It's dark. Definitely raining. Thunder at varying intervals fills the scene with dread. A lone man makes his way down a long corridor. He walks into a darkened room and picks up a clamping device of some sort. His face twists convulsively and a silent scream turns his face red. What is it he's found? A torture device? No. It's just your eyelash curler. But let's face it: we ladies have some weird crap floating around in our makeup bags.

And it isn't just weird crap, it's weird rituals. I mean, look at us! There you are, standing in a towel with a line of white goo smeared above your lip, a Q-tip in your ear, picking your face. Not so much? Well, maybe that's you, lying on the sofa, an open bag of Doritos splayed across your lap and the wrapper of a Reese's Cup somewhere in arm's reach, a small dot of choco-late lingering to the left of your cutest dimple. Or what about the girl stand-ing at the mirror, brush to mouth belt-ing out every word to Journey's "Don't Stop Believin'," shaking out her hair to every impassioned guitar riff? Not you? Sure. We believe you.

The major catch with living with the man you love is this: while you're supposed to feel close enough to reveal those weird things you do, at the same time, you are particularly interested in him loving you back. Of course, most healthy relationships can withstand the fact that you have to be home on Wednesday nights for *Wife Swap* or that you have a serious addiction to cheese that dispenses from a can. How-ever, private moments are private, not because we are the only ones who do these things—because, honestly, everybody does *some-thing*—but because they give us boundaries. They provide us with an identity and a sense of self. We all have both self-perception and an idea of how we'd like to be seen by others. Both provide

STRATEGIES FOR GETTING SOME PERSONAL SPACE
Politely tell him you need to be away from him for a little while.
Explain that it's good for you, mentally, to have some alone time.
Tell him you need to take a bath. And soak. And soak. And soak.
Start to meditate, pray, go for walks or otherwise remove yourself from his presence for just a little while each day.

us with an important sense of identity and even a semblance of control. In other words, it feels good to monitor some of our own behaviors. Letting go of that control can make us feel vulnerable and uncomfortable. But it's really not such a terrible thing.

"The mystery is over," says life coach Lauree Ostrofsky. "Emotionally committing is a bigger step than living together. It's another level. The more you let him in, the stronger the relationship. Remind yourself, you've already accepted *him* and go from there."

REASONS YOU SHOULD BREAK SOME PERSONAL BOUNDARIES

Letting him in could make for a stronger relationship.

You'll probably want to feel uninhibited in your own home.

REASONS YOU SHOULD KEEP SOME PERSONAL BOUNDARIES

You're interested in him actually liking you and not thinking you're a weirdo.

You're not ready to see all of *his* quirks yet, so you don't want to open that can of worms.

The fact is, everyone has moments that are left undiscussed. We're not saying this is nineteenth-century England and there are certain things that can be known only to you and your serving woman. Sure, we are of a generation that has no qualms about letting our clean undies dry from any protruding hook or knob in our apartment! And everyone has enjoyed Air Supply at some point in her life—well, okay, maybe not everyone. Still, the fact remains: some things are just . . . well, private.

"The reality of any given relationship is that the two of you get to design it just for the two of you. You can set your own boundaries," explains Ostrofsky. "If it is something that only affects you and you'd like to keep it to yourself, that is a boundary you can feel comfortable establishing."

Happiness and peace in your home rely deeply on your ability to feel comfortable in your surroundings, and feeling completely uninhibited in this place into which you lock yourself and your favorite stuff is vitally important for a solid, healthy sense of well-being. Of course, when there is more than one of you, a little compassion and cooperation are what create this harmony.

A few helpful tips from a non-romantic roommate perspective include Elyse's, who says she does her more private rituals in the privacy of a locked bathroom. She reserves dance parties to power ballads for Wednesday nights while her roommate attends her weekly French lesson. Meanwhile, Morgan, who grew up with four sisters and a brother, found ways to carve out privacy for herself, like knowing to belt out her favorite cantatas only in the shower and only with two loud fans blaring.

So maybe you don't want to show him right now how big you can puff out your belly while belting out your most off-key rendition of that song from *Rent*. That's okay. After all, someday you could be doing both of those at the same time while he's flipping pancakes wearing his ripped, faded high school football jersey and a faux hawk (what? that's what he does behind closed doors?)—and you'll love each other just the same. You and your boyfriend are always going to be more intimate with each other than non-romantic roommates and are therefore going to have fewer boundaries. Ready, set, burp.

Top 10 Behaviors Real Women Wish Their Guys Did Behind Closed Doors

10. Clip his nails.
9. Sniff his clothes to be sure they're clean.
8. Eat smelly food.
7. Fart.

6. Swear.
5. Burp.
4. Use the toilet.
3 Blow his nose.
2. Scratch his crotch.
1. Cut his nose and/or ear hair.

Gross and Grosser

Most guys will tell you, there are some things they just don't want to know. So your instinct to keep your feminine itch creams at the bottom of your makeup bag is a good one. By the same token, you don't necessarily want to know about whatever that stuff is growing in the duffel he takes to the gym. Of course, in time you will probably have to deal with each other's weird quirks and, er, fungal medications, at least to some degree. But, as with the weird stuff, unfurling the granny panties is more wisely done slowly, rather than chucking them at him as he walks in the door.

There are certain things you're allowed to keep to yourself. "I keep them in my hope chest under my grandma's afghan blankets," says Kate, a flight attendant in Philadelphia. "I have several things in there: all the pictures from previous relationships, old love letters, things I have written, and of course my vibrator—which I haven't needed since we started dating."

Believe us, he's a guy. He won't notice or think to look. Just know that if there are *many* secrets between the two of you, you should be asking yourself why. The women we interviewed who married their live-in boyfriends were the ones with the least secret stuff. In fact, most of them couldn't think of any objects they hid from their guys.

It's okay to give yourself a night, once a week or even once a month, that is all yours to do your grossest. Use it to do those things that really don't require an audience, like getting into it with those blackheads, sitting in a tub until you prune, or experimenting with spray-on self-tanner. Hopefully, on that night he is very far away. But if you know you won't get the house to yourself, make the most with what you have. Even if what you have is a 5-foot by 8-foot bathroom with no tub, set up a stereo to play any music you want and lay out your products. Make sure before you begin that you have all the

THINGS YOU MIGHT NOT WANT TO SHOW HIM RIGHT AWAY (BUT, SLOWLY, YOU CAN LET HIM KNOW THEY EXIST)
Feminine itch creams
Granny panties
Photos of old boyfriends
Love letters from old boyfriends
Vibrator
Voodoo doll that looks strikingly like his ex-girlfriend

towels, tools, and time to do all the activities you plan to do, from plucking to dyeing to drying, give it a duration and say to him, "Take care of any business now because for the next two hours you don't have a bathroom." Otherwise, there's the possibility he will find you, pants at your ankles, taking a moment to groom your bush. (You know you do it.)

After all, if this thing lasts you will end up seeing each other in a lot of the not-so-pretty moments. And some of these things will be messy. He will hold your hand while you give birth or you will hold his when he loses someone he loves. You will both likely be covered in runny snot at some point or something else runny and gross. There is plenty of time to unearth the dirt. But for now, it's still playtime. He is not your husband; he is your boyfriend. And there is nothing wrong with a little mystery. Dig slowly.

Separation Anxiety

Bodily excretions and closeted cosmetic-OCD aside, sharing a home with your boyfriend results in an inevitable bleed of your life into his. If the transition is smooth—fantastic, pat yourselves on the back. But chances are things will come up that deserve, if not an Atlantic Ocean of distance, at least a burbling brook of separation. For example, you may have a friend whom your boyfriend finds intolerable or who likes to discuss her sex life in detail with you. Even though you're not hiding your friendship or the fact that these conversations exist, you'd rather not rub it in his face. So how can you maintain relationships and behaviors you'd rather he not know about?

WHY YOU SHOULD ESTABLISH SOME BOUNDARIES EARLY ON (EVEN IF YOU LOVE SPENDING EVERY MINUTE WITH HIM)

It's important to have time alone with your friends, even if it's just talking on the phone.

An early precedent will make it easier for you to get time to yourself later.

Time apart diffuses tense moments.

Well, it's tricky. "Talk about your needs," says Calame. "You both might need separate time with friends. Explain your intention to go into a room and close the door to be on your own." True, we live in the era of the personal cell phone and e-mail password. Those two little developments in modern technology are truly our friends in maintaining our independence. But what if he's always home, looking over your shoulder?

June says she started going for walks the minute she moved in with her boyfriend. "Right off the bat, I established that I was going to be doing this every so often. While I was walking, I could talk to anyone I wanted to on my cell phone. It made it less awkward because I wouldn't have to explain myself or reiterate the whole sordid story if he was like, 'Wait, who did KC hook up with last weekend?'" she says. "I set the precedent because I didn't want it to seem weird when all of a sudden I was going to want to be alone."

Establishing certain boundaries early on isn't a bad idea. Try to anticipate your inevitable need for space and independence and make habits that he will come to expect. Walks aren't just good for phone time, they're also a great way to both diffuse tense moments and give you a chance to think in the midst of a disagreement. If you're a walker, he won't interpret your behavior as defiant, further exacerbating any uncomfortable situations. He'll just think you like to walk. Not to mention the bonus that after you've walked away from an argument and returned, you're in a better state of mind to discuss it. And, of course, a smaller ass.

A Thin, Reddish Line

Boundaries aren't strictly about the amount of space and the amount of alone time you give each other—they are also about letting yourself stay in control of your independent self. As we keep emphasizing, you are not married. Some things may rightly stay your own private experiences and information. Still, inevitably, you will learn a vast amount of new information about each other. After sharing all those new, formerly private moments together, he could become the one person in the world who knows the most about you.

That can be a really satisfying feeling—or really scary. Getting comfortable with your newfound proximity can be challenging.

The key is finding the right balance. For example, you still want to be able to hold hands with him while sitting on the couch—but certainly not *every* time you're on the couch!

SINGING IN THE SHOWER AND EIGHT OTHER (FORMERLY) PRIVATE ACTIVITIES THAT ARE BETTER WITH A PARTNER

Singing in the shower. Nudity + Music = Fun

Pigging out on pork rinds or on a carton of ice cream. Pick your poison. Your secret's out, so indulge together.

Watching bad reality TV. See previous entry.

Using a sex toy. Need we say more?

Reading. Sure, you can be in the same room in total silence. Swap books when you're both done.

Playing fetch with the dog. It's more like monkey in the middle. You'll be cracking up.

Killing spiders. Okay, so maybe this isn't a partner thing, and he can take over.

Doing crossword puzzles. He might help you with the answers you don't know. And you'll finally complete the Sunday puzzle.

Private dance party to Guns N' Roses. Hey, he probably loves GNR too. Go ahead and rock out!

But how do you let the closeness begin? Obviously you have made a commitment to each other as boyfriend and girlfriend. When you agreed to share a home, you let things develop even further. But now, as your belongings and hearts become increasingly intertwined, how can you accept the loss of many of these boundaries? How do you learn to share under such close emotional proximity?

The best advice is to begin by looking at your own behaviors, get to know your triggers, and communicate these to your guy. For example, you may be hard at work writing in your journal and don't want to be bothered. Then you hear his key in the lock and feel the hairs on your neck bristle with annoyance (trigger!), take a deep breath, and try not to have that fight you've been meaning to have about him leaving his coat on a chair at the kitchen table. Instead, give him a peck and hug hello and say simply, "Get comfortable. I'm just going to finish up a few things and then we can talk about our plans for later." It also might not hurt if both of you agree to leave each other alone for a few minutes when you get home from work, if that's what you need. He might find he likes it, too.

Usually you'll know that it's time to set a boundary because it just feels right. "When I'm IMing my best friend, I always take the laptop into the bedroom and close the door," says Theresa, a singer in Albuquerque, New Mexico. "It's not like I'm hiding my conversation from my boyfriend. I just feel like she and I have a bond when it's just the two of us and that's important to me." Like Theresa, you can simply create the boundary by removing yourself from the space your boyfriend is occupying. You don't always need to discuss the privacy issue—just make it happen!

We guess that you'll set a lot of boundaries in the beginning, but they'll evolve over time. Some will disappear: "I used to wear this disgusting purple face mask only in a locked bathroom," says Theresa. "But after five years, we've seen it all, so there's no point anymore." You may put up some new boundaries, though. Maybe you just can't handle the way the toothpaste dribbles down his chin when he brushes his teeth, and you decide to just leave him alone until he's done—for the sanity of both of you. Whatever works for you is okay.

Feeling Smothered?
5 Excuses That Will Snag You Some Alone Time

1. Take up scrapbooking. Go sit in the office with the E! Network on and a glue stick in front of you. We assume he'll leave you alone for this activity. (Frankly, we'd probably leave you alone for it too . . .)

2. You're having the girls over to watch the first season of *The OC* on DVD. Ask him if he could make plans with friends. Explain that the girls canceled at the last minute. Oh, no, you'll have to watch by yourself.

3. You have cramps. Works every time.

4. You're trying out a new self-tanner. You can't sit on the furniture, and he can't touch you. Perfect for some quiet time behind a closed bathroom door.

5. The oldest trick in the book: you're going to take a nap.

Your Own Private Idaho

"What tends to happen is that there are different ideas: One person wants more space. The other less," says Calame. So what happens when you differ on the privacy issue? "I've told my boyfriend a million times that I want to be alone when I'm taking a shower, but he still tries to come in sometimes," says Tiffany, a banker in Lincoln, Nebraska. "I've learned to get up early and take my shower before he gets up. That way, it's not an issue." You, too, may have to give in a little to make it work. It may be hard to accept, but you must adjust a bit to make things work for both of you.

Embrace your need for boundaries and respect the ones he puts up as well. "Talk about it," says Calame.

WHAT IF YOU DIFFER ON THE PRIVACY THING?

Be polite and express your desire for more or less.

Try to respect *his* perspective.

Adjust your behavior to try to make it work for the both of you.

Talk about it openly and honestly.

If you're the one who wants more privacy, remember that it's okay to let him in a little. You might just enjoy it.

"Don't let it go or someone could end up feeling suffocated and the other rejected." But understand that discoveries will be made by each of you in your time. It is a growing process for you as a couple and as individuals, and will ultimately inform the life you have together with richness and depth.

Don't forget, it will be important to get caught every once in a while, in front of the bedroom mirror doing an interpretive dance to "Making Love Out of Nothing at All." After all, the man's heart would have to be made of stone if that doesn't make him fall even more in love with your adorable self.

6.

your social and romantic life

My relationship with my best friend was on the rocks when I moved in with my boyfriend. I had always been the single friend and she had always been the one with the serious boyfriend. She had yet to move in with a boyfriend, so when I announced that I was taking that next step before her, it was a big shock to her. Prior to my relationship, my schedule was very free, so when I did get a serious boyfriend and had to work around that a bit, I could easily see her bitterness.

Before I moved in with my boyfriend, I lived only a ten-minute walk from my friend's apartment, so when I moved in with him—a twenty-minute drive from her place—there was definitely a problem. I remember her saying to me, "I'm not going to visit you when you move because you're the one who made that decision. You'll have to visit me if you want to see me." When I asked her if she was happy for me she said, "I'm happy for you, but I'm not happy for me." Mind you, she's an only child and we've been best friends for almost twenty years now, so there's a bit of possessiveness that comes into play sometimes.

—Carol, school administrator, Boston

The thing is, you love your friends. They have been there for every weepy phone call about every charming asshole you've met from high school to the European backpacking trip. They've hugged you when you've been dumped and helped you clean up your egged car when you've dumped him.

And now you've got it, the relationship to end all relationships. You call him Shmoopy and he calls you Baby. You are so disgusting that you want to proclaim your love from the rooftops. But you only want to go to the rooftop if he's standing by the chimney, or if you can see him from beside the chimney. Because, frankly, you love your friends, but . . . "What's that, Shmoopy? Did you say something, Shmoopy Moopy Woopy?"

You are in Boyland. And sometimes it's hard to leave.

Sarah says, "I used to stop by my friends' houses if I was bored, but now I have Jason to entertain me."

Cristina agrees, "I made him the center of my life and stopped making as much time for friends. He did the same."

It is a crime. We've all been victims of it, and, if we haven't already, might one day become victimizers. But the thing is, love is a mighty strong magnet. Sometimes it is hard to leave your man's side.

"I know that I never meant to become one of those girls. I hate those girls. But as soon as I fell in love it felt compulsive or like an addiction. The dude was my cigarette and like it or not, I was gonna smoke him. All the time," confesses June.

But then one day, you wake up in the home you both share, thinking, "It sure would be nice to have a friend other than Old Morning Breath over there."

Our advice? Do what you can to avoid abandoning your buds. They are part of what makes you independently you. "Something about you as an individual attracted him to you in the first place. Keep that alive," says life coach Lauree Ostrofsky. "Remember that no one individual can, in all fairness, be everything to you at once. With that often comes resentment and dependence." Duh, you need your friends too!

Need some strategies for making time for them? Carol says, "I found that having a girls' night, as cliché as that sounds, really works. Although I'd hate to say it's killing two birds with one stone, it really allows me time to see all of my good friends at the same time."

Sometimes killing those birds is a great option. There will come a point when you are honestly excited to get out and see your friends on your own, even if your impulse right now is to stay by his side. So for now, meeting up with friends on specified nights might be exactly the thing.

If your friends are single, and you simply *must* bring your guy out on the town, make it a group outing. Make sure other singles round out the pack. As Carol points out, "It's easy to see friends who are in relationships, as double-dating is always an option."

TIPS FOR KEEPING UP YOUR FRIENDSHIPS
Have a girls' night.
Deny your impulse to spend every minute with him.
Go out with him *and* a group of friends.
Make double dates with friends in relationships.
Spend time *without* him with friends who are having trouble adjusting to your relationship.
Know that it might be difficult for things to stay the same with your guy friends. But don't be afraid to try!
Sit down with disapproving friends and talk it out.
Encourage your guy to stay close with his friends, too.
Don't be afraid to tell your friends how much you care about them!

GIRLS' NIGHT IDEAS

Poker Night: Cigars optional.

Paint Your Own Pottery: You could also decoupage, build something out of wood, knit, or be otherwise Martha Stewart-y.

Cooking Class: Everyone makes something in front of the group like on a cooking show. BAM!

Potluck: Cooking class minus the cooking part . . .

Movie Night (In or Out): Ladies' choice, so it totally doesn't have to involve CG or slow-mo gun fighting. Unless you want it to.

Going Out Downtown/City-walk: Wear makeup and see if you can get hit on. Why not? No one's watching . . .

But what about those friends who disapprove of your relationship or who are having a hard time with the transition from single you to coupled you?

Carol notes that her best friend had trouble with her relationship at first, so she says, "I am always sure to give her at least some time with me alone. My boyfriend helps with this, so when she comes over, he sometimes goes in the other room to play video games, or at least tries to give us alone time."

Mel, a teacher in Cincinnati, ran into the problem of having to alter her relationships with her guy friends. She says, "Mark and I started dating and Morgan—a close guy friend for both of us—also started dating a really cool girl. We would all get together and Morgan and Mark would pair off and talk to each other all night while I talked to Morgan's girlfriend. I didn't mind, because I really like the girl, but I definitely miss the fact that the three of us aren't like we were. It's only natural that the boys remain closer but it makes me sad."

Amy says, "There was one friend who thought my interest in Ryan was temporary and was negative about us being together and getting married. But I sat him down and made him get the heck over it." Amy is definitely on to something. When it comes to making sure your guy stays close with his buds, make sure you do your best to make them all feel comfortable with you. But this advice can work even as you feel tension developing among your own friends. Telling people that you love them and value them is almost never unwelcome. Your friends can and want to hear from you, even from Boyland.

A Little Help from My Friends

In some cases it is harder to get him to keep up with his buddies, which in turn might make it more challenging for you to keep up with yours.

Jennie, a pediatric endocrinologist in Chicago, says that even though she really would like Jonathan to stay in touch with his pals, "It drives him crazy for me to bug him about calling his friends, and I have lots of friends who I like to see, so I just do . . ."

Amy says, "I wouldn't mind if he went out more . . ."

Sarah has a great solution: "I set up play-dates for him to make sure he still sees his friends, I encourage him to go play golf or basketball with them (plus it gets him out of the house so that I can have some alone time)." Establishing time away from each other and creating a life outside of your romantic world is healthy for both you as an individual and for your relationship.

MORE GIRLS' NIGHT IDEAS

Dinner Night at a Restaurant: Someplace nice. Don't skimp.

Jewelry-making: Download some ideas and go for it.

Slumber Party: Tell your boyfriends to get their minds out of the gutter: There will be no pillow fighting—well, maybe one pillow fight.

Bowling, Pool, or Darts: Remember when you did any of them without trying to impress the boys?

In-Home Spa Night: Hand massages and foot massages and doing each other's hair ain't just fun, it feels fabulous!

Picnic: They're not just for romantic outings. Take it to a park and get a little fresh air.

Paintball: Get rid of the aggression the old-fashioned way . . . by shooting at things.

Sometimes your boyfriend doesn't mesh with your friend group, or you don't mesh with his. The fact is, we look to a romantic partner for different things than we look for in our friends. We may seek lovers who are stalwart and protective, where in our buddies we seek recklessness and fun.

Cory, a comedian in Brooklyn, says, "I was freaked out that Jason never let me do my comedy routines for him. I could just tell it wasn't his thing. But I have a million friends who love to help me practice. So, I let Jason off the hook on that one. I know he'll make me dinner and rub my feet. My friends aren't lining up to do that!"

However, sometimes it is up to you to help your friends adjust to him and vice versa. "I have tried very hard to make sure Brian gets to know my friends since he moved to Columbus," says Courtney. "My friends have become his friends. I also think it is important that we spend time together and apart with our friends."

> ### TIPS FOR HELPING HIM STAY CLOSE WITH HIS FRIENDS
>
> Be encouraging. Mention that he should go out and give him the time to do that.
>
> Don't nag if he's not responding. Just see your friends, and he might get bored and call his own pals.
>
> Go ahead and call his friends and make plans, if he needs that motivation.

Even though we encourage you both to maintain relationships beyond each other, accepting and even becoming a part of each other's worlds is inevitable and necessary as well.

Courtney went on to point out, "One of the most helpful things is that Brian really likes my best friend's husband, so the four of us spend a lot of time together."

It is a good idea to nurture those relationships he comes to naturally. But otherwise, do what you can to blend into even those friendships of which either of you are initially wary.

"At first I was the only girlfriend, and it felt like I was breaking up the group," admits Colleen. "I made a point of going out with friends without Matt so we would get quality time. I would also go away for weekends without Matt for the same reason. Matt makes time for his friends as well. I pushed him to in the beginning 'cause I didn't want to be accused of breaking up the boys' dynamic."

TIPS FOR LETTING HIM INTO YOUR SOCIAL WORLD—AND GETTING INTO HIS
Let him get to know your friends. Spend time with them *and* him—and without him.
Hang out with other couples together.
Don't try to break up the group. Gradually blend each other in.
Give him his space—let him go out with his pals and do his thing.

If you trust your guy, you will let him spend time with his crew and embrace the alone time you get out of it . . . or the opportunities to see your crew.

Nikki says of her guy, "He thinks I am pretty laid back about his boys and appreciates that I don't give him a hard time all of the time like a lot of his friends' girlfriends do to them."

Keep It Date-y

Colleen pointed out in the last section that by going out with her friends, she and her boyfriend are able to maintain the allure of QT for them. But regardless of your social life outside of your love life, making sure you two are able to squeeze all the fun out of being a nonmarried couple will help your cohabitation be all it can. You aren't married. Don't act like it!

Nikki says, "We still make time to snuggle on the couch every night for at least fifteen minutes or so. Usually we snuggle and I fall asleep in his arms. Besides that we still cook dinner for each other and leave each other cute messages."

WAYS TO NOT ACT LIKE AN OLD MARRIED COUPLE
Cuddle.
Do nice things for each other, like cook dinner.
Leave each other love notes or send love messages.
PDA: Sneak kisses and hold hands.
Try to make your relationship a priority.

Hey, those are tips even The Marrieds could use. After all, a little PDA never hurt anyone. Nikki goes on to say, "He also always gives me little kisses or grabs my hand when we are out in public."

But what if you are busy? Here we are, reminding you to call your BFF and have dates with your boyfriend—and in a later chapter we're going to jump down your throat about cleaning up after yourself. What if you work? What if you have a nine-to-five job that is sometimes seven-to-eleven? What if you swear there are way fewer than twenty-four hours in the day?

Ann, a pediatric resident from Oakland, California, says, "He gets home from work late, often not until at least 9 P.M., unless I specifically ask him to come home earlier. And I have to get up really early, so we don't always see each other much during the week—I also sleep at the hospital every fourth night. I work a lot of weekends, and we both have traveled a lot this year for work or personal stuff but we haven't traveled together much."

The bottom line is, prioritize your relationship. As much as it needs space to grow, at the same time it is also vital for you to give it your attention.

Growing Daisies in the Doldrums

"We have a lot to talk about so I love spending time with him," gushes Lydia, an artist and stay-at-home mom in Los Angeles, California. "The excitement comes and goes in waves, but it's been four years so I think that's normal."

Colleen admits, "If anything ever gets me down, it's usually this aspect: yearning for the butterflies-in-your-stomach days."

But it is normal to fluctuate between the butterflies and boredom.

Ostrofsky explains, "Just like you aren't going to have a good day every day, neither is he. Sometimes, when you are feeling negatively, you have to step back and ask yourself what you want from the relationship overall. If most of those things are still there, it's probably safe to carry on."

Still, there are ways to keep things fresh. Carol and her boyfriend try not to just fall into another night at home. Instead they invite each other to spend time together as though it is an event. "I think labeling a normal night as a date night or a fun relaxing night makes the night something to look forward to," says Carol.

Mel, a teacher in Cincinnati, Ohio, and her boyfriend also swear by date nights. "After a couple months of living together we got in a rut," she explains. "Then, we made date night on Wednesdays. That way, we always know there is time set aside just for each other. It has

> **MORE STRATEGIES FOR KEEPING THINGS FRESH**
>
> Pick a night to call "date night" and plan to spend it together in a special way
>
> Balance your social life with your time with him.
>
> Value your time together.

helped keep us romantic. I definitely still get excited for date night and so does he! I highly recommend it."

A balanced social life is a skill you hone over time. Don't be too hard on yourself if you find your friendships and relationship redefining themselves. It is all part of life. Do your best to find time to show your friends you care. Let your relationship grow in the spaces between time together, but make sure you never undervalue that time together! As June puts it, "My grandmother once told me, You can't expect one person to be your everything! Feel free to have friends that fill in the blanks."

Ideas for Date Night

1. Go out for dinner to a cheesy chain restaurant and pretend it's one of your birthdays for a free dessert. Oh, and maybe you'll get a sombrero.

2. Go listen to live music. It can be more fun than a movie, and you can flirt!

3. Read each other a chapter of a book every night before you go to sleep. Hint: While Russian literature is awesome, Turgenev isn't really your best bet for reading out loud. Think Harry Potter or something with Fabio on the cover.

4. Catch a classic movie at an old local theater.

5. Um, Planetarium? Nuf said.

6. Put on your sexiest little black number and meet him at a fancy cocktail bar. But arrive there first à la Julia Roberts in *Pretty Woman*.

7. Eat-with-your-hands night. OR eat-with-his-hands night. Feed each other. No cheating.

8. Or, just eat in total darkness and see what's for dessert.

Creating Time (subtitled: Squeezing Blood from a Stone)

"One of the reasons we moved in together was because we were both so busy," says Anya, an advertising executive in New York. "But then we lived together so it was like we allowed ourselves to get even busier."

The thing is, just because you moved in together doesn't mean you can set your relationship to autopilot and assume time will grow out of your soundly sleeping snores. Anya made another key mistake when she and her boyfriend moved in together. Besides forgetting to include time for their relationship in her life, she also assumed that just being around him was enough.

"It wasn't," she said. "He moved out."

Relationships require more than a goodnight kiss. But what are you going to do? Sometimes there just isn't enough time. We've all been there. Especially if you are new to the work force, there are bosses who, no matter how many *Cosmo* articles we leave around for them to peruse, will never see a night at the movies with your guy trumping the Thursday deadline that they will remind you contains the word "dead" for a reason.

So how do you make time together? "Get ready to learn a little something!" says June, "Like about cars. I now have the most random knowledge about automobile designers because that's what he loves. So, there I was at car shows and auctions."

You can also turn it around on him. Teach him about something you love in turn!

Julie, a writer in Brooklyn, New York says, "He's such a dude I was embarrassed to let him in on my little obsession with show tunes. But after I did, he got really into it. He even bought me show tickets for us for my last birthday!"

By learning something about each other's hobbies and why he can't get enough of card games online, you will diminish even more distance between you two. You might create a more solid bond. And finally, you could end up building that elusive little life together you intended when you signed that lease in the first place.

Being the Teacher or the Student—With Your Clothes On

Teaching is an art form. Most school districts require a masters degree and a whole lot of time clocked as a student teacher. Suddenly you find yourself with this guy who you totally love but who is really all thumbs with a glue gun, and you decide, "Teaching him to collage with autumn leaves is destroying my love of crafting!"

It's a bitch, but seriously, don't be one. "It's really easy to adopt bossy tone," says Louise.

You want him to learn to love the things you love too. Especially if this is a way for him to become more involved in your life! But what if it just isn't working? "Let go, a little," recommends Louise who tried to teach her guy to ski. "When I did that, it was just cool to do our own thing together. It didn't matter so much that we couldn't do all of our runs together."

> **BEST TIPS FOR MAKING TIME FOR BEING TOGETHER, WHEN TIME IS OF THE ESSENCE**
>
> Don't assume living together is synonymous with building a life together. It still takes work.
>
> Make an effort to spend time together even after you move in together. Don't use it as an excuse to get busier!
>
> Learn about something he loves and spend time with him doing it.
>
> Teach him about your hobbies and passions and have him do the same with you.

Even if it might take some time to get the skill of your partner, or bring them up to your speed, like with Louise and her boyfriend, in the end they still got to drink hot chocolate and cuddle by a roaring fire. They didn't simply meet up on Sunday night before the workweek for a quick kiss before getting reabsorbed into their jobs. Which one sounds better to you?

But let's say it just ain't happening. Let's say no matter how sweetly you bat those eyes, he is not donning a leotard to join you for those weekly trapeze lessons. How do you create an extracurricular activity you can share?

SHARING INTERESTS AND KEEPING IT FUN
Don't become a "boss," if you're teaching him something new.
Remember that if the shared hobby becomes stressful, it's defeating the purpose.
Don't try to compete with each other—enjoy being at your own levels, separate yet together.
Enjoy the most fun parts together.
Choose an activity in which you both can express interest.

Wendy took a cooking class with her boyfriend. "Now we cook together once a week and it's also given us something to talk about that we are both excited about!"

Sit down and talk about things you've always wanted to learn or do. Make a list and see if there is any overlap or if something one of you has said sparks an interest in the other. Then go ahead and start a plan to learn about it. If there is no time for a class, maybe each of you can prepare some information for the week to discuss before bed. Then once a week, find a time for a practical application of your newly shared interest. Either look at a car engine together or buy a few stocks together to see what they'll do. Ultimately, you will be strengthening your relationship, which is as good as any bull stock, in our humble opinion.

sex while shacking up

When we used to go one night without having sex, we'd both get really stressed that something was wrong. Now that we live together, we sometimes go two or three nights without having sex. We always acknowledge that we want to, but with our busy lives and the fact that we live together, we can't always have the energy we did when we were dating and only saw each other a few times a week. Also, since we only saw each other a few times a week when we were dating, we always had sex, and the rest of the time we weren't together.

—Carol

It's Friday night. You and your guy have barely seen each other this week. He's been text messaging you all day long about the dirty things he's going to do to you tonight. You're so excited, you can barely concentrate on the road while driving home. I mean, it's been way too long since you two have had time for sex that wasn't perfunctory—and way too long since he's done his signature move, the Upside Down Reverse Donkey.

You get there and he takes you into his arms. Suddenly, there it is: that kiss you saw ten years ago at the movies that you swore you'd get one day. Your clothes are practically melting to the floor when . . . Wow . . . um . . . did someone blow up a stink factory? After you manage to stifle your gag reflex with a few hacking coughs, McGassy mumbles, "Excuse me." He swaggers toward you, without missing a beat. He loosens his tie, and continues kissing your neck. You try to get back into that horny state you were in only moments ago, try to think hot, heavy, raunchy thoughts. You look deep into his eyes and all you can muster is, "I think *Hairspray* is on Showtime tonight. I really want to see it." A single mention of a fat-suited John Travolta playing a woman and the mood is lost for good.

Sometimes the things we experience when we live with someone aren't exactly the makings of a romance movie. More like a romantic comedy with a few too many butt-jokes. Crotch scratching, stomach flus, head lice, yeast infections (which inevitably lead us back to crotch scratching), and of course, the morning after margarita madness at Chili's—none of this stuff is sexy. So how do you deal with being grossed out by the same person who's supposed to turn you on?

Remember what attracted you to him in the first place. "What about the relationship turns you on?" asks Lauree Ostrofsky. "If

HOW TO FIND HIM SEXY DESPITE GROSS MOMENTS

Remember what attracted you to him in the first place.

Think about all those things that still turn you on about him.

Find sexiness in the fact that you're closer now that you know all those gross things.

Focus on the fact that *you* can feel less inhibited in bed—you love him through all the grossness, so he'll love you no matter what, too.

Keep a sense of humor through it all.

MOVING-IN MANTRA: ON SEX

"Having sex is like playing bridge. If you don't have a good partner, you'd better have a good hand."—WOODY ALLEN

you think about your turn-ons and make your sex life a priority, you'll get there." Yes, he might seem grosser to you now than he was before, but that also means that you are closer, not only physically but emotionally, too.

"I think if you focus on things being less sexy just because you know more about the other person, you're missing out on a whole other level of being in a relationship," says Kerry. "I think in the mixing of our dirty laundry and other such things, we've seen an entirely different side of each other. It's not as raw an excitement as maybe seeing someone's underwear for the first time, but it's a closeness that I really love. Being completely comfortable with someone else is extremely rewarding, far beyond the more superficial first stages of being together. Sharing a certain level of intimacy—even in its grossest states—is something that I am very proud of and happy with."

So, while your inclination may be to mentally separate the disgusting stuff from the sexy stuff, the best strategy may be to embrace it. No, we don't mean that picking up his sweaty socks off the floor should turn you on. But knowing that you've reached a new type of intimacy, feeling more liberated in front of each other, could take your sex life to another level.

Like everything else, this works in reverse, too. Don't think you need to hide everything about you that's not-so-pretty in order to keep some element of perfect sexiness in the air. Life isn't perfect, and you shouldn't expect each other to be either.

"I don't believe in the philosophy of keeping the romance alive by hiding part of yourself from him, like never letting him see you without makeup or in your favorite ratty PJs," says Sarah. "The most unsexy look my boyfriend has is when he walks around in his underwear and wife-beater with his dark dress socks on. He knows I think this, so he does it on purpose, and then he sticks his stomach out and rubs his hairy belly. But it just makes me laugh."

Yes, a sense of humor helps *a lot,* too. Not everything has to be so serious.

Keeping It Hot

Even if your guy is the neatest, most hygienic person in the world, there are bound to be some changes in your sex life once you move in together. And even though most of the women we talked to wouldn't admit that their sex lives were changed *because* they were living together, almost all of them said sex was either less frequent, more tame, or both since moving in.

One big factor is that the relationship simply isn't new anymore. "I think when you are first in a relationship both people are releasing tons of hormones. In the beginning we were having sex like rabbits and every time was exciting. After a few years this wore off a little, but we still find each other sexy, which makes it good, but definitely not as exciting as all the mystery is in the beginning," says Samantha, a retail buyer in San Diego, California.

The other big factor is that, well, you're always together. Like Sarah and her boyfriend: "A lot of the excitement is gone when you know that you can do it anytime you want, and there's no roommate to sneak around. Plus you never have the question of if you're going to sleep over, and which apartment to sleep at, and then having nights apart, so that the nights together mean more," she explains.

Then there's stress, fatigue, and differences in working and sleeping schedules. What once came so easy when you two were starting to date, just may not once you live together.

Relationship expert Christy Calame suggests, "There is usually a drop-off in sex after you move in together. I usually recommend a book called *The Erotic Mind* by Jack Morin that mentions that sexual desire is increased by obstacles. These include parents, distance, and available time. Obviously, when you move in together or otherwise engage in a long-term partnership, many of these obstacles are removed."

So if you both are stressed, tired, bored, or just know you've already tried the Twisted Salty Pretzel and never need to go back there again, that's totally okay. The problems come in only if one of you feels unfulfilled, uninterested, or sexually disconnected. And if that's the case, talk about it! The only way he can know what you want in bed or vice versa is if you pipe up and just say it. This goes for kinky stuff, too. Seriously, talking can be all it takes.

"Talking about sex, even when we're saying we're too tired for it, usually makes both of us want to have it right then and there," says Aurora, an accountant in Baltimore, Maryland.

If you don't have the adventurousness of the sex life you had before the move-in, you may just need to freshen things up. Try a little role-playing if both of you are comfortable with the idea of it. Visit a sex shop together and pick something out for you to use during lovemaking. Come on to your guy while he's doing something mundane, like changing the oil in the car, so he doesn't see it coming.

"Now that things are more regular, we don't do any of the fun stuff like going down on each other. I think it is important to still incorporate those things into your sex life along with foreplay," says Gena, a professor in Washington, D.C.

All of these things can get you both very excited.

Calame reminds us, "Cohabitation is not the most erotic thing. That's why people do the vacation thing." Go ahead and plan a sexy getaway. Just remember not to put any liquids or gels over 3 oz. in your carry-on luggage.

REASONS WHY YOUR SEX LIFE MAY GET ROUTINE
The newness may wear off.
There are fewer obstacles when it comes to when and where you can have sex, making it less exciting.
Stress, fatigue, and differences in working and sleeping schedules interfere.
AND HOW TO SPICE IT BACK UP
Talk about your sexual desires.
Try something adventurous like role-playing or sex toys.
Be spontaneous—come on to your guy when he least expects it.
Make foreplay a priority.
Plan a sexy vacation.

Sex Games

We know. Sex is not a toy. But it can involve them! And when it does, it adds a whole new dimension of fun to your bedroom life. Now that you live together, are so good at communicating, and have gotten to know each other so well, we say, amp it up!

Of course, inevitably there is the following warning attached to this game (recommended for children eighteen or older): Sex should never be a tool to gain power. It should never be used to humiliate or belittle (unless previously agreed upon and accompanied by "safe words" so everyone knows when the fun has stopped). But here you are, living together, having a lot more sex than the single girls you know. You trust and love your man. Why not use this period in your life to experiment? Why not explore?

First of all, be prepared to step out of your comfort zone. "It took him a long time to admit to me that he hated it that I shaved 'down there,'" sheepishly admits Julie. In this case we'd advise Julie to let it grow to see where it takes her sex life.

Wendy isn't afraid to involve hardware; luckily, neither is her boyfriend. "The first time I proposed incorporating a vibrator I was really surprised at how widely he smiled!"

But if you want a more inexpensive, albeit equally noisy, option, you could always ramp up the vocals. Start with the heavy breathing and work your way into full-blown narrative descriptions. To do so, June advises using the phone. "As soon as he goes on a business trip or I am away for the weekend we bust out the phone sex!"

Pretty soon you can bring that audio into the bed. Try telling a story that turns you on. It can even be out of a movie you saw all told in the third person. This will get you talking. You can also tell him what you think of his body and feel free to steer clear of words that freak you out. But eventually, slip them in (gross!) but why not? Why leave the kinks to the bad hair days?

We also recommend role-playing—like that movie plot you just described? Act it out! If your guy is reluctant, start it off and see if you can slowly guide him into joining you. Julie says, "My boyfriend was a little timid with some of the things I like in bed, but after a few tries he got into some of it." See? The nice thing about living together is all that time you have to work it out.

Cecile also has some great advice. She says, "I'm pretty verbal about what I like, so we'll either tell each other, show each other, and/or encourage each other when we are enjoying ourselves."

For Kerry getting her boyfriend to turn her on at this point has more to do with giving thanks. "He has figured it out on his own, God bless him."

The 10 Best Ways To Revive A Dying Sex Life

1. Buy new underwear and then give him a fashion show.
2. Go someplace exciting together—on a hike or a camping trip. Physical exertion of one kind can often lead to other kinds.
3. Make a sex dinner. Include raw oysters and a whole chicken and a chocolate cake. And then forget to use utensils.
4. Give him a haircut. Or let him style yours.
5. Washing each other in the shower is great foreplay!
6. Dance party together.
7. Did we mention a haircut? How about finding hair to groom on other parts of the body?
8. Watch porn. You pick it. And yes, you can pick one with or without a story line.
9. Try doing some sensate focusing. Close your eyes and have him run his hands all over your body . . . without ever touching your skin.
10. Or try the same thing, but this time really touch each other everywhere except those places that really, really want it!

Sex Nights and Days

Second only to "What is the meaning of life?" the most common question for couples is, "How frequently should we be having sex?" When you can tell us the meaning of life, we'll hit you with the secrets to copious amounts of endlessly fabulous sex. Everyone's different and every relationship is different, too. Christa, a librarian from Detroit, Michigan, says, "There are some days when all we do is have sex." While Ruby, an artist in Silver Springs, Maryland, explained, "We end up having sex one or two times a week, but I wish it was more like three or four. Our schedules don't seem to allow for that, though."

STRATEGIES FOR INCREASING HOW OFTEN YOU HAVE SEX
Have an appointed "sex night."
Agree to have sex when you don't feel "in the mood." You'll get there.
Wear a sexy outfit.
Watch movies and do things that excite you together.

If your frequency isn't living up to his or your expectations, making an appointed "sex night" where you traditionally do something special and then have some great between-sheets time afterwards. It may be all you need. We know that a sex "routine" doesn't exactly sound romantic at first, but experts say that anticipation can be a big turn on. Just looking forward to a date night may be all you both need to be rarin' to go.

A women's magazine once suggested that when women get comfortable in a relationship, they want to have sex less and would rather find physical intimacy in other ways like cuddling, whereas men want to have sex just as often as they did before. Theresa has a similar theory: "He's up for sex a lot more than me," she says. "It's annoying how the female sex drive is so much more affected by the emotional state." We're not sure how much we buy all that battle of the sexes mumbo jumbo. I mean, as we mentioned before, every relationship is unique. In fact, Amy countered, "I'm more often ready for action than my guy is."

What we will say is, one of you will probably want to have sex when the other doesn't at some point in time. The important thing is that you're each sensitive to the other's desires. If he's getting annoyed that you've been too tired all week to knock boots, you could make an effort to at least try. We know you can muster up the energy for one little romp. You may find out that once you're in the thick of foreplay, you definitely won't want to stop. And if you're on the other end of things, and feel like you always have to convince *him* to do it, try to be understanding. That new high-pressure job may be taking its toll. When you get a chance, try some new moves to turn him on. Amy's recommendations for keeping things interesting for both partners? "I try to spice it up every once in a while. I love hotel sex. I would recommend getting sexy outfits, watching movies that excite you, and doing things that are a rush because that can translate to the bedroom."

Try skiing or surfing. Even if you're not a daredevil, doing something together like playing a sport or going for a bike ride together will be a bonding experience and get both of your hearts pumping. And those bodies bumping.

Non-Porno Sex Scenes to Turn You On

Some are romantically erotic. Some are just plain flaming hot! Pop in whichever one you think will get things smokin' at home.

Pretty Woman (1990): You don't see much, but Julia Roberts and Richard Gere do it on the piano keys. Now that's making beautiful music together.

The End of an Affair (1999): Maybe it's just us, but we're getting all worked up thinking about the way Ralph Fiennes's ass moves while he's sticking it to Julianne Moore.

Secretary (2002): Maggie Gyllenhaal gets spanky with her boss, James Spader.

8 Mile (2002): Sex in public places—even in the back room of a factory, like it was for Brittany Murphy and Eminem—is hot.

A History of Violence (2005): Viggo Mortensen, Maria Bello, a cheerleading uniform and the number 69 all play big roles in one particular scene.

Unfaithful (2002): Okay, it isn't exactly a pro-commitment sex scene but good lord, that Frenchie works some magic with Diane Lane in the book stacks, oh, and in the bathroom stall.

A Walk on The Moon (1999): Because Diane Lane is cheating on her husband again but this time with Viggo Mortensen. And it's hot. Again.

Sex and Lucia (2001): Sometimes you have to peruse the foreign films to get your dirty sex with the tasteful art house vibe. No one even has to wear dark glasses!

Yup. You've Lost that Loving Feeling

It doesn't take the Righteous Brothers to point out when the flame is dying. But the good news here is that usually it doesn't take all that much to turn it back on. Sure, now you know each other's less attractive nooks and crannies. But you also have a deeper connection that can spark some lovemaking like you never thought possible!

Even if Judith isn't feeling it, she says she can always get going with some simple smooches. "Kisses, hugs, kisses and kisses," she says.

For Hope, it's a little more complicated than that. To get her in the mood she advises, "Offering to get me my favorite ice cream and telling me I will not have to do anything so I can just relax."

"Give me a back rub!" says Maggie.

Sometimes it takes more effort than he is willing to put in. "When we moved in together our sex life changed. I hate it when he just cannot take the time to get me in the mood!" says Almudena, a translator in Burlington, Vermont. In a case like this, it really doesn't hurt to have a candid conversation about how he can help you get in the mood. Seriously, he knows what he wants, so be a pal and help him out! After that conversation, you can shut the hell up and enjoy it. Like Almudena says, "Luckily, most of the time you don't need to talk, right?"

WAYS TO GET IN THE MOOD WHEN YOU'RE SO NOT

Lots of kissing!

Relax! He can help you with this by doing something nice for you or giving you a back rub.

Take the time for foreplay.

Dare him to get you in the mood.

By no means should any of us be having sex out of obligation. If you aren't in the mood, tell him. But we recommend you put in the following caveat: "Go ahead and try to get me in it!" We think you'll be glad you did. Dianna agrees. "If you just get started you'll always be glad that you did." Remember, she goes on to advise, "It doesn't have to be a space shuttle launch every time but it's important to make the time for it and put in the effort."

Letting Him ... er ... Down

Perhaps you are feeling less sexy more often these days because you are in situations where the question of your sexiness has had a chance to come up more often. Before, when you weren't really feeling it, you had a place to go and hide. Now he might want it, and there is no place to go. You don't always have to give in, but let him down gently. After all, sexuality is fragile and we all feel vulnerable when it comes to sex. Try to avoid phrases like "Get the hell off of me" or "I am so disgusted by you right now." Harsh words might get him off you for the moment, but then it might just keep him from getting back *on*.

Almudena says, "I try to tell him directly, but I have to control it so that he doesn't feel I am being too bossy."

Just choose your words. There is a reason "I have a headache" has become a joke between couples. But it serves its purpose. It takes the responsibility off of him. Unless there is some long-term problem in the relationship, sometimes pinning the blame on your mental state or other things happening in the world is a simple way to politely decline the advances without declining the man. After all, it's not because he totally repulses you, so you don't want him to start thinking that you do.

Hope suggests, "Promise 'getting some' in the very near future. Like an IOU. Then stick to your promise."

Another way to get out of it avoids speaking altogether. "I usually just fall asleep," says Kerry.

But again, turning turning-him-down into an art form isn't the best way to live your life. Lauree Ostrofsky says, "Making your sex life a priority means making your sexuality a priority, too.

Connect to what turns you on, about yourself and him, and you'll get there." Just try not to "let him down" more often than you let him . . . um . . . up.

sticky situations: pets, roommates, holidays, and more

My roommate and boyfriend did not get along and they often put me in the middle of squabbles. It was very stressful and difficult. In the end my roommate started acting weird and distant and we were arguing too much, even though her boyfriend had moved in, too. There was too much tension so I moved out and in with my boyfriend.

—Samantha

Living with your guy sometimes means living with other things—a roommate, the Labrador he rescued off the side of the road that just can't seem to learn not to pee on your hand-made rug, the rare orchid he bought that needs to get three-quarters of a cup water each week but no more or less (and to face a westerly window). Or even, most importantly, a son or daughter. While all four of these living things require their own, distinct handling, what they all need is an agreement.

If you haven't moved in yet, this is the time to discuss how the situation will be dealt with—by both of you. If you already live together and are thinking, "D'oh!" it's never too late to broach this subject.

Roommates

It's common to have to live with a roommate along with your guy, because of a financial situation, a lingering lease, or, well, because you want to be nice and not kick her out. The first thing you should do is look into getting your own place with your guy. And nicely tell your roommate that this is your ultimate plan. This will help you avoid the issues that are bound to crop up when you're sharing your space both with your guy and a roomie.

"My then-boyfriend—now husband—and my roommate didn't really get along all that well. I mean, there were no major clashes or anything, but theirs were totally different personality types," says Erika.

We know what you're thinking: My guy is amazing and my roommate's not so bad either. This isn't going to be such a bad thing. Well, of all the women who said they went through this situation, none of them said it was all kittens and rainbows.

"It wasn't that difficult, but it was more chaotic and it was definitely a relief to only live with each other," says Lindsey.

And in the meantime, until you get your own place together? Be nice and respectful. Make sure she still feels comfortable in her own home. Sometimes when you're single, it's hard to be

TIPS FOR LIVING WITH ROOMMATES
Start looking into moving out as soon as possible.
Warn the roommate early that this is your plan.
In the meantime, be nice and respectful. Make sure everyone is as comfortable as possible.
Avoid making out in shared spaces of the home and doing other things that would nauseate your roommate.
When you're ready to move out, *kindly* explain your plans to your old roommate.
Give her enough time to find a new roommate or make other plans.
Make sure your financial obligations are paid up.
Offer to help your roommate find someone new to move in or find a new apartment.

around couples, let alone *live* with a couple. Remember that when you're dealing with your roommate. Try not to make her uncomfortable by doing things like making out on the couch when she's at home or taking showers with your guy, and try to include her in social activities. Invite her to the neighborhood bar to have a drink every now and again.

"We tried to keep our time in public spaces limited and hung out in my room a lot or went out. We tried to be careful not to offend my roommates," says Dianna. "It was their place before mine anyway, and they did introduce us, but nonetheless we didn't want to be impolite or put anyone out."

Then, when you and your boyfriend find your own place together, explain to your roommie that this is important to you and your relationship. Make sure you've paid all the rent and fees you've agreed to—it's not right to stick anyone with a lingering lease. Or offer to help find a new roommate to fill your spot. It's the right thing to do.

Plants

Plants may seem like inanimate objects to some people. But to others, they are living, breathing creatures. Actually, they totally are living and breathing, but some people really don't give a shit about plants. And maybe you and your guy have opposite views on this subject. No matter. Just make sure you have agreed to disagree—and agreed what your roles are in the plant's life. You want to take turns watering? He wants you to keep your hands off his precious bonsai? Be sure you've reached an agreement you can both live with—and stick to. If you don't trust him to keep your orchid fed, then make sure you're taking on that responsibility solely on your own. Because, even if you love your living, breathing plant, it's not worth fighting over.

Animals

Animals not only live and breathe, but they eat, shit, sleep, cry, visit doctors, and have daycares—they even stay in their own hotels, and wear designer clothing. Seriously, there are dogs and cats that live more luxuriously than some humans we know. Some people will even argue that pets are capable of love.

Sometimes, disliking or not tolerating a partner's pet goes unsaid. In the case of Dianna, her boyfriend avoided telling her that the cat she'd inherited was literally making him ill. "Josh was so sick, for three weeks, with the worst cold and sinus infection. I begged him to go see a doctor. He broke down and told me he's really allergic to cats! He was afraid to ask me to get rid of the cat, because he thought it meant he'd have to get rid of his dog, Dozer. He didn't want to live without Dozer or without me, and the best solution in his mind was to suffer for the rest of his life!" Turns out, Josh should have spoken up sooner. Once he admitted his allergy, Dianna admitted that she never liked the cat ("you'd have to meet that cat to understand," she says) and gave it up for adoption the following weekend. Remember that honesty isn't overrated.

You might be surprised to see what either of you is willing to sacrifice for the sake of each other. Jeanette explains, "He had a bird. I *hate* birds. It hated the sound of my voice and would scream whenever I was around. Not to mention the fact that its food had moth eggs in it. It was so gross! I was really honest with him and told him I couldn't live with a bird—especially one with moths. He got rid of the bird. I know it was hard for him, but it was a deal breaker for me, and he wanted a deal."

Of course, the solution isn't always getting rid of the pet. Sometimes, especially in that case of people who've had the pets so long—or love them so deeply—that they're a package deal, one partner will have to grin and bear it, and maybe even change their ways. Gail, a store manager in Lansing, Michigan, says: "I have the dog and he hates it. Not really the dog, but the dog hair. I tell him that the dog was here before he was and that the dog will be here after him—I also advise him not to make me choose, that he won't be happy with the result."

TIPS FOR LIVING WITH ANIMALS
Be honest about your love, hate, or allergic aversion to the pet before moving in.
Be prepared to give away a pet for each other.
Be open-minded about each other's pets. You may end up falling in love with his.
Remember that some people think of pets as family.
Take responsibility for a pet he's not enthused about and do the walking and feeding yourself.

If your guy doesn't deal with dogs well, it's okay not to part with Spot. But don't expect your boyfriend to feed or walk him. Maybe in an emergency, when you're stuck late at work, but, really, he's making a compromise for you, don't make him take on a responsibility he doesn't want.

Kids

Kids are, of course, a whole different banana. Actually, they're the whole banana tree and all the little bananas they've spawned. Kids are a big deal. If you or your guy is bringing kids into the household, there is no division of labor, no trading off responsibility, no way to ignore their best interests in favor of your relationship.

We're no parenting experts, and we think you might need an entirely different book for this topic, but we will say that being a parent is a big part of cohabitation. According to the U.S. Census Bureau, 41 percent of unmarried-partner households have children under eighteen living in them, and about two-fifths of all American children are expected to live in a cohabiting household at some point. You're not alone. If there is one thing you can take from our spiel about the plants and the pets, it's that you should have a plan in place. Know what role you're going to take in the kids' life—and what your man's will be, too. Even if his children visit every other weekend, the fact that you're sharing a household with their daddy makes you a stepmother of some sort: someone who will take care of them, someone who will act as a good example they can look up to, and someone who will possibly become a disciplinarian. Be prepared for this, even if you aren't planning on marrying the guy.

And he should know to endorse your role. Lorna, a nurse in Sioux Falls, South Dakota, says, "My guy was great in that he never interfered with any disciplinary action I took with his kids. He was very supportive of me and made it clear to them that his relationship with me was important to him." Lorna's best advice? "Make certain you know what his stance will be with you and with the kids. We clearly defined expectations, together, then sat with the kids to discuss them."

TIPS FOR LIVING WITH KIDS

Be in agreement with your boyfriend on how parental situations will be handled.

Remember that the live-in partner will be like a stepparent in many ways, and be sure you're comfortable with that.

Be prepared for huge responsibility.

Pick up a parenting book and consider family therapy if it is a cost you can incur.

Gear up for quite an adventure.

Seriously, we won't go on and on about this one—even though we totally could—but Tina, a lawyer in Madison, Wisconsin whose cohabitation situation involved kids, says this: "Make certain you know what you're getting into. Know how you're going to handle this. There will be issues; there will be problems. Don't kid yourself." And then do the best you can—because that's all that any of us can do.

Questions More Difficult than "If We Don't Have a Chimney, How Will Santa Get In?"

There are other sticky situations when it comes to living with him. I mean, you're sharing body fluids and your morning English muffin—perhaps not at the same time—but when it comes to celebrating the holidays, you're not technically family. Some of his family might not see you as family either.

So do you celebrate together or not? Well, each couple's situation is totally unique, so take all the factors you can into account. First, maybe you don't even feel ready to dye Easter eggs together just yet. Maybe you want to wait until you are closer to marriage or more deeply committed.

"We celebrated separately the first year, but after we got engaged, we went everywhere together," says Lisa. "Our families live very far apart, and at the beginning, neither of us wanted to give up our own family celebrations."

If you'd rather wait until marriage or engagement, that's fine, but most of the women we asked said they celebrated holidays with their guys.

"I think if you're serious with each other you spend holidays together, regardless of your marital status," says Lindsey.

Of course, just *how* serious might affect your decision whether to break bread as a couple. "If your intention is to build a family together, then yes, you should start acting as a family and make sure that holidays are spent together. That's what family is about," says Dianna. "If living together is not about building a family, then spend them apart if you like."

Another big factor that might come into play? Proximity—if your peeps live close to his peeps, it could be really easy to see both of your families in one day, making it a no-brainer that you'll spend the day together party-hopping. "We went to both [of our parents'] homes, together," says Laura.

Before you decide to do this, you may want to consider how your family views your relationship—if they're not supportive, think twice about bringing him. Even if they love your boyfriend, make sure it's okay with Auntie Sue that there will be one more head for her annual Roberts Family Free-for-All Gift Swap.

Remember that your unmarried status may mean that you or he isn't *always* invited. "When we first started dating I was not invited to his older cousin's wedding that I was hoping to attend . . . Since then I have attended many weddings and bar and bat mitzvahs for his family's events." says Hope. Try not to get offended—often for big events like these, the hosts have to stay beneath a specific head count, and "dates" for unmarried guests are often first to go (as completely unfair and outdated as it may be—depending on which side of the checkbook you fall).

If for some reason one of you doesn't feel welcome at the other's family bash, you might want to avoid that situation to make the day enjoyable for everyone involved. You might want to share the morning of the holiday together in your own way, then split up in the afternoon, and then when you come back together do a little, um, clothing-free celebrating. Remember that if there isn't a reason *not* to celebrate together, and you want to, you should totally do it. Dude, you're an adult now—sharing the holiday makes it your thing, not Mommy and Daddy's. Create your own rituals, whatever they may be.

"I never spent the [actual] holidays with the boyfriend I lived with," says June. "But every year we'd set up a tree together and decorate it. We'd make hot chocolate with Kahlua and then sit together and just stare at it."

Laura agrees that you should celebrate together, in your own way. "Then it becomes your own tradition, not someone else's. 'Never live your life for others; live it for yourself' is what I always tell people," she says.

SHOULD WE CELEBRATE THE HOLIDAYS TOGETHER?
How serious is my relationship with my boyfriend?
Do I envision us as a family now or in the future?
Would I prefer to wait until we're married (if that's in our future) to celebrate together?
How easy is it to see both our families/friends while spending the holiday together?
How do our families/friends view our relationship? Are we welcome at each other's family/ friends' celebrations?
Did I/he check with the party host that it's okay if he/I tag along?
Is there a way we can spend the holiday—or at least part of it—together without involving family or friends?

I'll Be Home for Christmas

Now, let's say your families live in different areas and you're forced to choose one or the other. In some cases, proximity can make your decision where to celebrate easy, as it did for Carrie.

"His family lives all over the country, and since we rarely get the day before or after the holidays off of work, there was never any real discussion of where we would spend the holidays," she says. "I always thought it was nice that he spent the holidays with me."

But in most cases, it can be subject to debate—one that Mom, Dad, and Grampa Carl might try to get in on. "Splitting up holidays is really hard. It's a point of contention," says Lindsey.

Some great solutions? First, make every effort to make it fair for both of you.

"It should be 50 percent of the holidays with each family," suggests Almudena. "You need to decide that together." Okay, so fifty-fifty is the ideal, but it may not be a reality.

One way to strive for equality? Take turns with all the major holidays. Next year he'll get Christmas with his folks, but this year, he gets Thanksgiving. Don't count holidays that are usually spent with friends, or doing nothing at all—like New Year's or . . . hmm . . . Flag Day. (No offense if you love Flag Day. Flag Day doesn't count.)

Consider all the holidays and choose the ones that are most important to your family or to you personally and try to compromise with him, letting him have his favorites. Naturally, consider what's important to him, too.

"Holidays were determined by family rituals and how important they were to each of us. I'm Jewish and he's Christian, so Christmas was with him, no problem . . . Passover was always with my family." says Cecile.

Dianna has a similar plan: "Easter will be out of state with my Mom since his family doesn't celebrate the holiday and it's important to me and my Mom's side of my family."

Consider other personal matters, too, when deciding where to celebrate. "I have divorced parents and grandparents, so that doubles the places to visit," says Lindsey. Take each unique situation, handle it with care, and do the right thing for you and your relationships—with your guy and with the loved ones with whom you normally celebrate.

It might even be a good idea to invite everyone to *your* place for some festivities. "One Thanksgiving, we invited both our families over to our place for dinner. His decided not to make the trek, but mine came and we had a nice time and neither of us felt guilty about not making an effort to spend the time with our parents," says Charla, a veterinarian in Weirton, West Virginia.

Make your best effort, but give it some time—this whole holiday thing might take a while to work out.

"We are not in a total routine yet," says Courtney.

No matter how fair you try to make your holiday plans, deciding to celebrate with one of your families and not the other can be an emotional situation. Many of us have sentimental attachments to the way our families spend the holidays. Say, to you, Christmas means a big shiny ham with plenty of au gratin potatoes in Aunt Fanny's quaint little condo with only your nearest and dearest. Well, then, celebrating over Cream of Sum Yun Gye at the local mystery-Asian restaurant with, well, people you barely know might not feel at all like Christmas. But give it a shot. You might turn out to like some of his clan's traditions, like the way he helps his nieces leave out cookies and milk for Santa. Sorry, but that's just really cute.

"Neither my family nor Scott's is religious, but his family liked going to the Christmas Eve service at a nearby Episcopalian

HOW TO DECIDE WHERE TO SPEND THE HOLIDAYS

Consider proximity for holidays when you have limited time to visit.

Make compromises to try to be fair.

Take turns with each of the major holidays.

Choose based on which holidays are more important to each family.

Take your family's individual dynamic into account—divorced families may require extra care.

Consider inviting everyone to your home on a holiday.

Allow time to figure out what works best for the two of you.

Be open-minded about how his family celebrates.

church to sing," says Erika. "I enjoyed going with them. It was a way to share something that they all enjoyed—singing carols."

"Being with his family at the holidays is part of getting to know the culture and traditions of the extended family at really nice times of year. You learn so much about a family during time spent with all of the generations together," says Hope. "They'll share the stories of the family's history and how everyone came to be who they are—including your significant other."

Remember that how you deal with the holidays could say a lot about your relationship: How serious you are about the future. How you share, compromise, and resolve conflict in general. How generous you are to one another and how much you respect who each other is and where you come from. Think about it.

chores and household duties

When we started living together, I was always cleaning. It was only a couple weeks before I had a fit . . . He would leave his shit—food wrappers, socks, the phone, dirty dishes, bottle caps—all over the apartment. That drove me crazy! Then for a while, I would ignore it and not clean it up to try to teach him a lesson. I thought for sure he would catch on when his crusty rice bowl was sitting there two days later. The problem was, he didn't catch on. His mess would become like part of the furniture, and he wouldn't even realize that he had left it there two days ago. Seriously, it was as if he didn't even see it.

—Mel

We all know there are more important things to argue and stress about than a clean house. But the thing is, there are now two people to clean up after—double the dirty dishes, double the junk mail to sort through, and double the soap scum to scrub off the shower. We've done it: trying to beat the spry couple who live down the street to the Laundromat—because eight weeks of laundry requires a minimum of five machines—followed by trying to endure the 104-degree heat produced by all those dryers.

After all that folding, not to mention the lugging of the laundry bag back up to your five-story walk-up, you hear him say, over the sound of his Xbox game, "You forgot my navy polo."

If that doesn't make you scream, you should consider becoming a professional poker player.

Chores suck. Even if you like doing them, you probably don't like doing them for other people, and while you're on your hands and knees wearing rubber gloves, smelling the stench of whatever filth you're trying to eliminate, it's easy to get mad.

Hannah, a high school teacher in Jersey City, New Jersey, says of her guy: "When I'm cleaning behind the toilet bowl I resent the hell out of him."

However, Hannah goes on to point out that it works both ways. She says, "All one of us had to do was say, 'I'm just going to vacuum a little here . . .' [and] it's as if the person who was calmly sitting on the couch enjoying the afternoon suddenly morphs into a pig rolling in his or her own filth . . . Tag. You're the slob for not noticing the place needed vacuuming."

So how do you handle the mopping and dusting without starting to loathe each other? First: accept the fact that you will have to clean up after each other. Second: hire a maid to lighten the load.

"We had a cleaner who came every two weeks to take care of dusting and vacuuming. I'd say having a cleaner is one of the best ways to reach relationship harmony. Yes, it's expensive, but I'd rather give up lots of other things to afford a cleaner," says Mindy, a writer and editor in Dobbs Ferry, New York.

But, okay, so yours isn't an Imperialist home in Calcutta in the 1920s. Fine. Not everyone can afford a cleaning person, emotionally or financially. It remains our sincere belief you *can* make this work. It's called division of labor. Talk about the things that need to be done around the house, and devise a plan that will work for both of you. Lauree Ostrofsky, our resident life coach, advises that sometimes it is best to adopt a middle-school test-taking approach to labor. "Eyes on your paper," she says. "In other words, sort out who does what and then trust each other to carry it out. Remember that it isn't about what he is willing to do, but what you are willing to take on."

When you hear his side of things, you might even realize that he does a lot more around the house than you give him credit for, like taking the cars to the shop, cleaning out the gutters, and doing the grocery shopping. This is not the time for coginess. Admit it if trimming bushes ain't your bag—maybe he'll volunteer to take on that chore, or at least do it half the time.

Often it can be really helpful to have had at least one solid conversation about what you expect of each other. If it doesn't happen naturally that he just always takes out the trash, you might want to make standard rules: "I wash. You dry." "I take out the trash, you clean the toilet." And so on. Ostrofsky concurs. "Have a frank conversation about how you envision your home. Make clear what is important for you and elicit the same from him. Then the divvying up happens and the sharing happens."

HOW TO AVOID ARGUMENTS ABOUT CHORES
Hire a maid if you can afford it.
Accept that you both will occasionally clean up after each other.
Discuss your expectations.
Talk out who does what—he probably does more than you think.
Divide up the chores based on what tasks you both hate least.
Be honest about what you don't like to do—he may be game for it.
If one of you isn't pulling his/her weight, reexamine the arrangement.

"Do what you like to do, and divvy up the rest," agrees Laura. "When it comes to dishes, I love washing, I hate drying. My guy loves drying; he hates washing. When we first moved in together he washed and I dried because we both thought we were doing the most hated task. One night I told him how much I hated drying and that he should be happy that I did that part, and he told me how much he hated washing. Talk about sacrificing for love. To this day, I wash, he dries and we are both happy."

In other words, don't try to be too nice—we know you're in love, but doing a chore you loathe for the sake of not pissing someone off becomes less and less romantic the more you have to do it.

June attests, "Once Neal and I agreed on our jobs around the house it helped me to stop freaking out that he never cleaned the bathroom. I just made a point to never take out the trash or do the dishes."

What to do if those dishes begin to pile up? "You may have to go back to that bigger conversation and reiterate your needs," says Ostrofsky. "But also check yourself. If you act like you assume it won't get done, rest assured, it won't."

Cleaning Is Messy

Make a routine. Every other Sunday, you might agree to clean the whole place together, or each of you agrees to do a little each day. We're not advising a construction paper chore board titled "Ship Shape" in the form of a boat with movable anchors naming daily tasks (although what a helluva colorful addition to the fridge!). It's also okay if every other Sunday slips into monthly. Do whatever it takes to make sure things are fair and getting done to both of your liking. Not everyone is on the same page as far as how often the toilet needs to be scrubbed (once a week; two if you never lift the seat) or how often the sheets need to be changed. In fact, Colleen found she had to verbally remind her guy to do his part:

"I tried leaving it till it was really dirty, but I would still give in and clean it myself before he took action 'cause I couldn't stand it anymore. Since then, I've learned to accept the fact that if I want him to help, I'll need to ask or to point it out to him."

Be honest and open with each other about your expectations. "I have so many friends who get annoyed with their boyfriends because they don't cook, pick up groceries, or plan meals, and I say, 'Well, did you ask him to?'

> **HOW TO MAKE SURE THE CHORES GET DONE**
>
> Make a cleaning routine and try to keep to the schedule.
>
> Be sure you're on the same page about how often things should get done.
>
> Don't expect him to read your mind. Tell him when something needs to be done.
>
> Be honest when you want him to pitch in in a new way.
>
> Be forgiving. You're not perfect either.

Inevitably, they say, 'No, I just thought he'd think of it,'" says Mindy. "No one is a mind reader. Be a big girl and say what you want, such as, 'I'd like you to plan and cook dinner two nights a week. It would mean a lot to me if we could share the meal thing.'"

This isn't something you *have* to establish up-front—you can broach the subject any time you want. You may be surprised at his reaction. Sometimes we're not aware of what we're *not* doing and need it to be pointed out to us.

June admits, "Because I didn't really grow up with chores, I kinda never thought about how the garbage got thrown out.

I just never did it. It took my first college roommate to point out that garbage, in fact, does not walk outside to the dumpster!"

You see, sometimes it isn't just that people are idiots. So while you are sympathetic to his lack of cleaning knowledge, accept that you might be missing some metaphorical dust bunnies yourself. After all, did you respectfully wrap up your used maxi pad before throwing it away? You didn't? Was that before or after you flipped out about his toothpaste blob left in the bathroom sink? Yeah. That's what we thought.

Evolution of the Single-Celled
Organism . . . in Your Refrigerator

Remember that your designated duties could change over time, as your live-in relationship evolves. Inevitably you will learn about each other. For example, Ariel, a real estate broker in Springfield, New Jersey, made the following discovery: "When we moved in together, I thought I should cook the majority of the time—maybe that's because I'm a woman, even though I'm a total feminist. I would get really stressed out if I burned something or if it didn't taste right. Then, one day when he decided to cook, he was dancing around the kitchen having a great time. I realized he really loves cooking. Now it's his duty."

Ariel's preconceived idea that it was her job to cook (and cook like everyone's mother in the Heartland of our most romantic

traditional gender roles: how do they apply to you?
They don't! As we said before, choose chores you don't mind doing, not what you think "The Little Mrs." should do.

American ideals) comes from traditional gender roles. That is one place
to start if you aren't sure what position
you will best fill in your new state of
cohabitation. He might be the lawn-
mower while you darn the stockings.
However, you might really want the
lawn-mowing exercise and he might
find darning swell. We are not afraid
to remind you that you don't have to
adhere to any rules, archaic or modern. Just find your groove.

"He vacuums, does the dishes,
and does laundry while I refinish the
kitchen table with the new power sander I bought," says Mel. "We
just look at chores as work that needs to be done and we do it."

> **SO YOU THINK IT'S FAIR . . .?**
>
> An MSNBC survey asked men and women if the chores in their households were performed by just one person or if they were shared. Figure out for yourself exactly what these results mean:
>
> 74 percent of men said the chores were shared.
>
> 51 percent of women said chores were shared.
>
> 26 percent of men said one person did the housework.
>
> 49 percent of the women said the same.

Neat vs. Clean—There *Is* a Difference

During all those years of singledom, you were used to things
being a certain way—maybe you prided yourself on the way you
tossed your dirty thongs around the bedroom all week long, but
cleaned them all up in one quick, hopeful Friday-night spree.
Or perhaps he liked his blender kept spotless at all times, poised
crumb-free for the next protein shake, nary a seed from a diet
strawberry smoothie to mar its pristine state. No matter what your
day-to-day cleanliness habits are, his are probably different.

Erika found that if she wanted the laundry to be done on
a reasonably regular basis, she had to do it herself. "I don't like
to wear the same pair of underwear for two days and then go

commando for another two before thinking, 'Hey, I need to do laundry!' I'm exaggerating, but still . . ."

But they may be less noticeable differences than that, like the difference between neat and clean—and messy and dirty. "We are both neat in our own ways and messy in our own ways," says Dianna. "He is not very concerned with piles of mess, and I can't stand that. I'm not concerned with deep cleaning, whereas he runs the vacuum daily . . . It's not an area where we're compatible, but it's not a deal breaker." She makes a good point—this is a common difference two people in a couple can have, but it's something that doesn't make you totally incompatible.

Nikki has a similar predicament: "I am what I like to call a scrubber," says Nikki. "This means that I am not afraid to get down on my hands and knees and really mop the floor. As a matter of fact I don't feel that a mop would clean it nearly as well as I do on my hands and knees. This is where we differ. He 'surface cleans,' as I like to call it. He will tell me he swept the floor and I will look at it and go 'Really?' Because I know what he actually does. He takes a piece of toilet paper and scoops up the hair on the floor. No broom, no mop. So he surface cleans—if you can even call it that, since it doesn't even look clean."

Don't get frustrated right away. Express yourself, of course, but give it some time. Sometimes, we're slobs simply because we're slobs, not because we're trying to hurt each other or make the other person do all the filthy work. You never know—with time, one of you might even adapt to the other's way of life.

"I was the messy one and felt obligated to clean up my act. Gradually, the tides turned and I outdid him in the neat-freak competition," says Hannah.

Acceptance is also a big step toward keeping the household harmonious. "I think you have to learn to live with and accept the little, insignificant things and realize that for everything he does that annoys you, you probably do something that bugs him," says Erika.

Like Erika, you could simply take on the tasks that aren't his forte yourself—really, is it that big a deal? Remember that while the object is to create a household that's fair, that may not ever be completely possible. The fact is, you might find that the energy it took to wipe the stubble off the bathroom sink is way less exhausting than that which you used for seething over three days as you watch it accumulate and merge with dust, fingernail clippings, and toothpaste. Just wipe it up already! Concurs Dianna, "No it's not 100 percent 'fair' in my house, but life is not all about cleaning."

> **HOW TO DEAL WHEN YOUR OPINION OF "CLEAN" DIFFERS**
>
> Sometimes you have to do something yourself to get it done right.
>
> Let him take on the jobs that aren't your forte.
>
> Lay out each of your expectations when it comes to the cleanliness of your home.
>
> Give it time. He may adjust. And you may, too.
>
> Know that 100% fairness is probably unreachable.

Room for Improvement

You may have lived with roommates before and had no problems—or had *major* problems. Either way, know that living with your guy is going to be way different. How?

Well, when you lived with a roommate, you were each responsible for making your own bed, cleaning your own bedroom, and cooking your own food. Now it's all shared. But it goes further than that. You and your guy will probably have more rigid expectations of how well-maintained the home should be now that you're living together romantically. The "nesting" instinct may set in, like it did for Mel: "We lived together as friends in college and we were both terribly slacky on chores. Our house was the typical gross college house. We have both come a long way and appreciate each other's effort!" she says.

Depending on how you work it, you may have a much better experience dealing with chores and the like with your guy than you ever did with a roommie. Ever had a roommate you let walk all over you? You probably won't be as afraid to pipe up to your guy about pitching in. "I probably let my guy get away with less than I ever did a roommate, because the friendship's not at stake. He loves me unconditionally," laughs Colleen.

> **HOW CHORES ARE DIFFERENT WITH BOYFRIENDS THAN WITH ROOMMATES**
>
> You share a bed, food, etc. No clear divisions here.
>
> You'll probably feel more domestic when living with a boyfriend and want to make more of an effort.
>
> Often, you can express yourself better to a boyfriend than you can to a roommate and might even tell him what to do.
>
> But you might also be more forgiving of his slip-ups.

Marnie, a chemist in Ann Arbor, Michigan, agrees: "It's totally different—I do more than when I had roommates, and I ride him more than I would a roommate." So you might be able to tell it like it is to your guy, but you also may be more forgiving to one another when you slip up. "I let him get away with lots. He's not a roommate, he's a boyfriend. I take care of him and he takes care of me," says Dianna.

Now, living with your guy *and* a roommate at the same time—that's a whole other soufflé. Because roommates don't necessarily feel like a team, the way a couple does.

The problem with adding roommates to the mix: communication. "We did live with another roommate in the beginning, and my boyfriend and her drove each other nuts with the cleaning. He thought it was disgusting that she would leave her dishes in the sink for days without rinsing them. She didn't like that he would shed body hair all over the bathroom. However, neither of them would tell each other and they both wanted me to be the mediator, which I refused to do so it never got dealt with," says Nikki.

Unfortunately, you might have to mediate. If your boyfriend moved into an apartment where you already lived with a roommate, or if you and the roommate began as better friends than she and your guy, it might just be the simplest way to keep the peace. It isn't always fun to be the hub of the wheel, but at least it allows people to say what they need to say. Chances are, your guy may not be comfortable telling your roommate how he feels the same way he can tell you. Same goes for the roommate. Best idea is to suck it up and be the messenger—even if in movies they are always the first to die.

CHORES. BOYFRIEND. ROOMMATE: HOW TO DEAL WITH ALL THREE

Try to communicate with everyone.

Do some mediating if need be.

Use your boyfriend as your ally. Maintain a united front.

Try to be fair when you can.

Make sure you and your guy are pulling your weight—you're two people not one.

The good news is that when you live with other roommates, with your boyfriend on your side you have an ally. "If I thought my boyfriend Mark wasn't doing his part in cleaning, I could talk to him, but it was harder to talk to the others. He also had to listen to me bitch about cleaning the bathroom for the third time in a row," says Mel.

If you two are living with a roommate, knowing the situation is temporary might help you get through it. That, and each other.

Power in Numbers

Remarkably, the thing that can often be the cause of most of your problems when living with an additional roommate might also be your saving grace: Your roommate(s) are up against two. We say, embrace the notion of Power in Numbers. It is similarly good practice for the rest of your life. If you find one of your boyfriend's requests unreasonable, maintain a united front in front of the roommate and tell your man privately how you feel. Make this practice known to him and see that he reciprocates. Then you will see how easily your shared household stays under control. (And by that we mean, *your* control.) But be fair. After all, your poor roommate . . . well, she should get to hold the remote control *sometimes.*

However, dividing up chores in the case of multiple roommates can't include the two of you equaling one. Even if your man moved into your space and the roommate predated him, he must pull his weight. If you plan on compensating on his behalf, cleaning the bathroom two out of three times and the like, make sure your roommate knows that you have cleaned on his behalf. Inevitably this will minimize problems like the roommate feeling like your team is not pulling its weight.

Then (again) start looking for a place for just you and your guy—the roommate thing gets way too messy.

Tips for Quick Cleans that Are Also Green

"I always take out the recyclables when I need to make it feel less cluttered in my kitchen," says Ariel. "For some reason, bottles and cans accumulate on the counter and it feels good to get rid of them all in one fell swoop. Plus, I hear it takes way more energy to produce a new bottle than it does to turn an old one into a new one."

Clean the shower while you shower!

Cecile in New York says, "I'm a fan of reusing plastic bags from stores for garbage instead of garbage bags and using cloth towels instead of paper towels."

Use old t-shirts for rags and simultaneously clean out your closet while cleaning the toilet!

Move to Vermont, suggests Almudena in Burlington, "I live in the kingdom of ecology. Everything they sell here is environmentally friendly!" or just buy green cleaning supplies wherever you live!

Or do green cleaning like Kerry in New York, "Procrastination uses less cleaner."

communicating with your guy

On our first date, I told my guy to know three things about me: (1) I was always right, he was always wrong. The sooner he learned this, the easier it would be for him. (2) My money was my money and his money would be my money. It was all my money. (3) I am a bitch. To this day, we laugh about this because he never took those comments seriously until we moved in together. By then it was too late. When he tells me today that I am being nasty to him, I remind him that I warned him on our first date, and he just chose not to believe me.

—Laura

Some relationships in your life require more formal dialog than others—and roommates and boyfriends are two of them. So obviously your cohabitation experience with your man just might double the amount of necessary conversation time. "Once you get through the heavier conflicts the mundane stuff comes up," points out relationship expert Christy Calame. "Is there fairness in chores? Luxury versus necessary purchases. What constitutes enough savings and what is too much debt? Even very wise people don't always anticipate what conflicts will arise."

Make time to talk. Lindsey from Brooklyn says, "I think there needs to be an open channel of communication when it comes to basically any topic. Of course the big issues are money, sex, work, etc. but you need to talk about everything."

As you live together and feel each other out you may learn that there are certain times and places that are most conducive to having a productive conversation about something that's bothering you—or any serious issue. Sometimes it is good to establish a time of day for talking.

"Avoid talking as soon as someone comes home from work," advises Lucy. "I find Ryan needs at least thirty minutes to himself to wind down after work. During that time, anything I bring up could make things hairy. Plan for a meeting time once a day, maybe after dinner while getting the dishes cleared."

Marie, a special education teacher in Philadelphia, Pennsylvania likes to capitalize on the cuddle time after sex to get into the good stuff. "I feel like I have his undivided attention. Really, I can talk to him whenever, but I know sometimes when I talk about normal day-to-day things, he just acts like he listens, but when we lie in bed together we can talk about our relationship and our future together."

Capitalize on those specific situations where talking is easier. Dianna from Baltimore says, "I like our road trips. We start a topic, think of it, talk about other things, come back to the original topic, it's nice."

Intimate locations like cars can be a great place to have deeper conversations. But remember that cars are bad places to argue. Place a "fighting ban" on the car. If a topic heats up, it is better to put a hold on it for a time where heavy machinery isn't involved.

But a solid and meaningful conversation with a little mood music coming from the crappy CD player can otherwise go off like gangbusters on a Sunday drive. June says, "We recently spent an hour in a car talking about how we want to raise kids. I mean, we had like three hours to kill, so why not?"

Jeanette points out that sometimes it is important to listen even when it's, well, fake listening. She pointed out, "Women need to talk and know someone cares, we don't want a fix all the time: just a venting session. We just need an ear to beat. Thus the act of 'fake listening' saying 'Yeah!' and 'Really?' makes us feel so good."

TIPS FOR TALKING IT OUT
Avoid stressful times, like right when you get home from work
Be sure there are no outside distractions.
Don't argue in the car.
Listen when he brings something up. Let him vent.
Remember to try to be on each other's side.

Want him to do this for you? Learn to reciprocate. One up him in your fake listening by asking pertinent questions in addition to the pensive head bob and the offhand "You're kidding."

Jeanette goes on to warn, "Make sure you like listening to your partner's stories. If your relationship is going to last, you are going to hear a lot of stories." Probably over and over and over . . . trust us.

Laura suggests the following: " Keep each other up to date, in the loop, and it will help keep you both on the same track." There are any number of obstacles you and your guy could face: family issues, friend issues, home issues. As long as you're in each other's corner, you can get through it.

You can't always anticipate what conflicts will arise in your relationship until you are in the middle of them. The best you can do is to take particular notice of the big stuff and try to head it off at the pass. Points out Christy Calame, "Cleaning, money, shared or not, people will always discover new areas of conflict."

Flogging Dead Horses

"Too much talking happens when the relationship doesn't need to be changed in the near future and you are talking and talking about where it's going for no reason," acknowledges Hope.

So, while it's important to talk, *yes*, there can be too much of a good thing when it comes to communication. Sometimes it is best to let it lie. If he is never going to put down the toilet seat, you may have to soul search on this one, but is that a reason to give up the fabulous foot rubs he gives? In other words, a never-ending dialog on why you may or may not fall in the toilet is really going to do far more damage to your relationship than just looking at the seat before you sit. This is not us letting them win the toilet seat war, because, seriously, we have all done battle over this one. It is just knowing when to let it go—and this goes for more serious matters, too.

Laura advises, "If you keep rehashing the same subject over and over, without resolution, this becomes a problem. Make a decision and move on." Dianna agrees, "If we belabor any point it's a drag for both of us and not in the least bit helpful."

Lauree Ostrofsky agrees: "One, rehashing doesn't serve the couple because after a while one or both of you will tune out and you will likely never get past it. Neither of you will be active in the solution. And two, rehashing doesn't serve you, by yourself." Ostrofsky points out, "We rehash usually because we ourselves haven't really gotten to the bottom of why that topic is important in the first place."

The same goes for any repetitive conversations or topics of conversation. June mentioned, "I compulsively brought up his ex-girlfriend in casual conversation. He humored it but it drove him a little nuts."

If there is something you are bringing up too often, try to figure out why you might be doing it. Are you feeling insecure? Jealous? Try to spot what it is you are trying to gain and then see if there are other ways for you to get it. Don't be surprised if you discover that this one wasn't even about him! Do your best not to muddle the issues in your relationship.

"Go deeper into the topic," says Ostrofsky. "If it's not about this thing, what's under it?"

As Wendy put it, "Sometimes you put drama in your relationship because you are just kind of bored. But that probably isn't where you want your drama."

A good way to avoid cluttering up your relationship might be to *not* talk about it—so much, anyway. Be sure you are talking about enough other

REASONS TO LET IT GO AND STOP REHASHING
It's not an important subject.
It's not getting resolved through repetition.
You may both tune it out after a while.
You haven't gotten to the bottom of why it keeps coming up.
You could be adding needless drama or clutter to your otherwise happy home.
Quiet can actually be good for the relationship, too.

things. Share hobbies you *do* together that you can talk about later. If you don't share many interests, maybe there's something you'd love to teach him about? He might seriously get a kick out of offering his input on a short story you're working on for your creative writing class. Or ask him to show you why he spends three hours a day on the computer. Find out what he does at work. When you find you are running out of reasons why his nose is so cute, figure out something else to discuss. Or learn to coexist with a little quiet time here and there.

"You get a chance early in the relationship to ask why a person is so quiet," says Ostrofsky. "If they tell you they are thinking, or just zoning out, believe them. Then don't ask again. Usually we want to break the silence because we don't trust why it's there."

Ultimately, your relationship requires a balance between talking about your relationship with an ability to chitchat about baseball, the weather, and his coworker's hair color—and sometimes, not even talking at all.

Them's Fightin' Words

Fighting happens. All we can do is hope that when it does, it stays manageable and ends with a clear and practical resolution.

"A lot of it is in how you present your argument," says Dianna. She suggested that comments like, "You leave those dirty socks on the floor for *me* to clean up!" and "You think that I'm your personal maid!" imply that these frustrating behaviors are a personal attack on you when they are not. People don't always see things the same way. His avoidance of the scum around the toilet bowl is more likely laziness or forgetfulness—or grossed-outedness—and not a message that you deserve to be scrubbing his shit off the toilet. (Boy, the damn toilet comes up a *lot* in this book! Sorry.) So it is safe to knock that off the list of reasons you are angry. Try not to imply it when making your stand.

Dianna advises that a better way to address the issue might be to point out the problem and create room for a conversation about it. Try stepping away from the toilet for a half-hour, calm down, then bring up taking turns doing the scrubbing in a toned-down, rational manner. "I think that if you are just more aware of your phrasing," she says, "it can really make a difference between healthy and damaging communication."

Lindsey and her boyfriend incorporate modern technology into problem solving. She says, "Google or imdb.com can usually solve most of our arguments!" Go with that if trivia is the source of your disagreement.

Hope advised, "Sandwich anything negative with two positives. Balance anything very serious with two lighthearted and funny things. Like an Oreo cookie!" Yum! Who can argue with chocolate, creamy goodness?

Be careful you don't bring up too many issues in one fight. In other words, never view a fight as a moment to bring up every grievance you have

TIPS FOR FIGHTING FAIR
Try not to make personal attacks, or even imply them.
Don't always take his actions or lack of action as an attack on you.
Point out the problem and create room for a conversation.
Wait until you're calm before you bring up the problem.
Avoid unhealthy or damaging words.
Use an impartial party (like a reputable Web site) as a mediator, if you're disagreeing on a specific piece of trivia or fact.
Try to infuse humor and positivity into your discussion.
Focus on this argument. Don't bring other issues into it.
Don't put down his family or friends.
Look for a resolution.
Try writing down grievances and talking about them later.
Remember that it's hard to take insults and harsh words back.

ever had. You were able to get over the skull constructed out of Christmas lights on the front lawn by New Year's. Why rehash it now, during this Fourth of July fight over what pie to bring to the picnic? Also, Laura advises, "Never drag his family into it; after all, the other party has no control over their family's actions."

Ostrofsky points out that it's easy to lose the thread of a fight if you aren't clear about its goals. "Having a successful argument means there is a beginning and an end," she says. "If you just argue from topic to topic you don't get what you are looking for, and that is some sort of resolution. You just get to be mad. And mad doesn't really serve anyone."

And while it's good to hash out these subjects, sometimes, when it's not that important, don't be afraid to find the humor in it and move on.

Sarah says, "When I pout, he just goes out of his way to make me laugh, and then it's over."

"Sometimes we would make light of the situation and start to tickle one another," mentions Lucy. "Great diversion."

She also suggests writing things down for him to read later. "No interruptions," she says, "or competing for air time."

Actually writing is good for everyone. It helps you clarify what you mean and gives you a chance to say it in an effective way. You can retain control instead of letting emotions muddle your point—or can simply vent on paper and rip it up later if you know you are being stupid. After all, once you've let on that you think his mother's drinking habit has been passed right along to him, when you just wanted him to change the light bulb . . . well, let's just say, some things are really hard to take back.

Passive Aggression and Plain Old Regression

Keeping explosions to a minimum doesn't have to be an impossible feat. The question is, how do you prevent a little spark from igniting a WMD? The biggest culprit is often passive aggression, or those "subtle" behaviors meant to alert your man to the possibility that you might be angry or frustrated. This is, of course, in lieu of an outright announcement that you are just plain disappointed and wish you weren't the only one who didn't pretend mildew is invisible. (It isn't. It is green and it grows in grout. But they invented a way to get rid of it! It involves a spray bottle and a little elbow grease.)

Passive aggression is often the result of a desire to avoid confrontation. As Jeanette speculates, "I think it happens because we don't want to 'rock the boat' because some things are really hard to talk about."

When this happens we start to exhibit behaviors that, frankly, make no one's life easier. We leave dirty dishes in the sink for days on end. We have a laundry standoff until we are washing our underpants in the bathroom sink and hanging them on every available towel hook.

Lauree Ostrofsky says this about passive aggression: "It is a tactic, like arguing, for getting what you want. However, the more articulate you are about what you want, the better the chance you have of getting it, and getting specifically *it*."

Otherwise, you might just get some of it, or none of it. The fact is, pouting is way less clear in the end than "Can you please do some laundry?" Right?

Regina, a veterinarian in Greenwich, Connecticut, says, "One time I was really mad at him about something, and I had left piles of his clean laundry on the bed for him to put away. I picked up the laundry and threw it all over the floor while he was in the shower."

The problem with this method of persuasion is that it is just as possible that he will end up doing the laundry as it is that you will walk into the bathroom only to find him drying his hands on your bra—actually, now that we think about it, the hand-drying thing is totally possible. Him picking up on a subtle hint and spending the day separating whites from colors? Nope, not possible.

Dianna learned this very quickly. She says, "[My boyfriend] would ask 'Are you okay?' and I would respond, in a huff, '*Fine!*' . . . he really would take that as 'I'm fine, honey bunches' and move on." What Dianna really wanted was for her guy to ask again. She wanted him to lead to the solution on his own. But ultimately, since she didn't clearly communicate her feelings, nothing was solved and perhaps the issue got lost, or worse, blew up later.

Are You Saving These Dishes for the Maid?

Other ways we "imply" our anger, rather than placing it on the table, include the silent treatment, withholding sex, or combinations thereof. Danielle says, "The silent treatment has been an effective way of letting him know I am pissed off . . . and no sex just naturally goes along with the silent treatment." Still, Sarah points out, "No sex hurts me more than it does him."

> **AVOID PASSIVE-AGGRESSIVE BEHAVIOR**
>
> Don't expect him to read your mind and "know" why you're pouting.
>
> Try to talk about it, in a civil way, even if you're not sure how to bring it up.
>
> Remember that he may deal with anger in a different way, so he doesn't *get* what you're doing.

Toby, an investigator in Columbus, Ohio says, "There were times I went on a laundry strike. But the strike didn't last long because I am a sucker and I felt bad, ended the strike, and did the mountain of laundry because I know he works hard."

Courtney uses the silent treatment but went on to say, "He also gets 'the evil eye.' He calls it 'being in the doghouse!'"

In Jeanette's case, her methods include: "No eye contact and single word responses: yes, no, fuck off . . . okay, that was two words."

These behaviors have the ability to hurt far more than heal, despite what you learned from your mothers or the ladies of *Dallas* and *Falcon Crest*.

Take note of other stressors that could be causing your frustration. It is a really good idea to take a look at what has triggered you (say, he hasn't taken the garbage out in two weeks and you are staring at a fat roach). Now consider what else is going on (like, maybe you just got a big folder on your desk at work with the word "Urgent" in red at the top). Now, make sure you calibrate your garbage response based on the awareness of the looming, Urgent folder.

Regina notes, "Part of it is that you're closer to this person than anyone else, so while you're hiding the fact that you're stressed at work from everyone at work, you don't feel inhibited about being grumpy around him."

Stressors can be hard to spot. Perhaps you haven't been sleeping great. Maybe your cycle agitates you at certain times of the month—but if he ever suggests that that's the cause, you deny, deny, deny. There are finances, a sick dog or friend or family member, personal disappointments and unmet goals. Sometimes traumas from years ago ignite seasonal irritability.

The chances of one being able to list all the stressors in their lives the same time they are facing Mama Roach ain't good and border on impossible. So as an alternative we advise that you always assume that somewhere in your life there is an Urgent folder, and go easy on the attack—in fact, try not to make it an attack.

Egging His Car Because He Forgot
to Grab the Mail Ain't Cool

Lucy mentions the time she lost it: "Ryan and I were living together for a short time, when the bottled-up frustrations erupted with me throwing a large head of broccoli at him as I was cleaning it up for dinner."

Needless to say, she went on, "It got my point across!"

Laura in Pittsburgh had a similarly aggressive meltdown. "I did break a chair over the dining room table in a fit of rage."

Anger in our culture is often equated with all things loud and violent. But these things tend not to be incredibly effective in terms of problem solving.

"But anger and aggravation are part of you," reminds Lauree Ostrofsky. "Let it out. Anger is there for a reason. So first, recognize your anger, then later, articulate it."

There are ways to acknowledge when you are meeting your breaking point. For example, blood very clearly boils. The heart rate quickens. You feel your face flush. Your breath shortens. Any one of these is a sign you might want to step back.

Toby says, "Usually my chest starts to tighten and I get so frustrated that I cry. At that point, I need to remove myself."

We recommend going for a walk or taking a time out anytime you feel a head of broccoli in your hand, poised ready to hurl toward the head of your man. Calmer conversations inevitably

how not to flip out

Know what stressors may be exacerbating your bad mood and alter your behavior to take it into account. Then be nice.

have far more staying power and lead to a healthier relationship in the long run, even if they lack the wallop of hurled produce.

"Of course, after the anger it is easier to figure out what you want," says Ostrofsky. "Express it then." Chris, a landscape architect in Cleveland, Ohio takes the following approach: "I take deep breaths and ask myself if it's worth arguing over. It usually isn't."

Laura went on to say, with regard to her broken chair, "I realize how childish that was. Aggression when fighting with a loved one is never the answer."

DIFFUSE ANGER TO PREVENT BROKEN CHAIRS . . . AND HEARTS
Find a healthier way to show your anger than throwing or damaging something. Articulate it.
Recognize the warning signs. If you feel yourself ready to flip out, stop and take a deep breath!
Take a walk to ease some tension.
Later, calmly bring up your feelings.
Ask yourself whether it is really worth fighting over.

Taking Liberties with the Breakup Threat

Okay, so you didn't get married. You have still made a commitment. Now you have a responsibility to that commitment. It isn't only because it is so much easier *not* to break a lease or divide up the '80s record collection. It's because you still owe it to your relationship to be careful what items you put on the chopping block during fights —the relationship should rarely be one of them.

"I am a spazz," says June. "I go from 'you never know what I want to eat!' to 'therefore you don't love me' in about five seconds. Next, inevitably comes the sullen decision that we should probably just break up."

Often one of the biggest falsehoods in fighting is that using the threat of breaking up might somehow strengthen things. The fact is, it only breeds insecurity and an overall mistrust in the relationship. Further, it is flat-out lazy. It sucks not to feel 100 percent satisfied 100 percent of the time, but inevitably you will not. That's an easy truth to forget when you are confronted with an empty refrigerator and the sinking feeling that if you stay in this thing he will never, ever remember to buy the milk.

"Everyone has a beast," points out Wendy. "You have to choose the one you can live with."

Christy Calame advises, "Making idle threats like 'We're breaking up!' can often end up feeling like a manipulation to your partner."

Katka, a film translator in Prague, says of commitment, "There are always exits in life. If you and your boyfriend stand around pointing at them, you'll never get comfortable."

Not everything is a test. In fact, *most* things aren't a test. Let's put it this way, if you aren't sitting in a room with fluorescent lights, two number-two pencils, and a Scantron sheet in front of you, assume it isn't a test. You are together because you trust this person to not steal your shampoo or insult your mother. So he doesn't want to watch your favorite TV show with you because he hates crying surgeons giving blow jobs in broom closets? That is no reason to pack up your china and head for your sister's sofa. Have a talk first. See where that gets you.

Reading the Nonverbal Cues

Communication in any form is a pretty huge part of any relationship. Sometimes it takes a lot more conversation. In other cases,

MOVING-IN MANTRA: ON COMMUNICATION

"Words are a wonderful form of communication, but they will never replace kisses and punches."—Ashleigh Brilliant

a lot less. Sometimes a couple just gets it. They already have some deep connection that makes it so no one has to bat an eye for harmonious garbage removal. They hear "I love and support you" in the wind blown around their partners' heads and words never need to be spoken at all. But how? How the hell do they do that? Sometimes it is so hard to know what you yourself want, how can you read his mind?

WHY YOU SHOULDN'T THREATEN A BREAKUP IN THE HEAT OF AN ARGUMENT

It breeds insecurity and mistrust.

You probably don't mean it.

He could see it as you trying to manipulate him.

It could disrupt the comfort in your relationship.

It won't solve the problem.

He might say "okay."

You can't always, but there are subtle physical cues that are pretty clear indicators of how your partner is feeling. Frankly, it is as important that you acknowledge these as it is to acknowledge the blatant expressions, like when Romeo says, "See how she leans her cheek upon her hand? Oh that I were a glove upon that hand, that I might touch her cheek!" You know what that means, right?

Hope says moving in with her guy helped her to recognize how he showed her he cared about her without speaking. "He takes care of things for me that he knows I would not enjoy doing. And he also comes home with presents for me all the time. He is a shopper."

By noticing the physical cues, you are well on your way to getting to know your boyfriend in ways even his mother never could! "He has a look that tells me he is loving me at that moment, while actually thinking about how he loves me," says Kerry in New York.

Dianna notices, "He tells me about his day, shares his feelings with me, and chooses to do things with me. He invests himself."

HOW HE TELLS YOU HE CARES WITHOUT SAYING A WORD
Bringing you gifts
Looking at you in *that* way
Choosing to spend time with you
Cleaning the house or doing a chore without you asking
Holding your hand or rubbing your back
Offering to get you a drink, snack, dessert

Cecile points out, "The nonverbal cues work both ways, learning to read when he needs space, when he wants to be together, and how to say I love you to him is also important."

It's true that you need to be on the lookout for signals that he might need things from you: and no, we don't mean a beer. Well . . . *maybe* a beer. But sometimes that silent treatment might not mean that he is suddenly doubting his love for you. It might just mean he needs you to give him a little space. The same thing applies to you. Learn to recognize when you are in need of a little quiet time and find an effective way to communicate that. Moving in together affords you a great opportunity to learn a lot more about each other. So take advantage like Kerry did with her guy. "He knows my weird habits, and I know all his faces and mannerisms."

But we'd like to bottle the following nonverbal cue: Almudena says, "If I am in a bad mood or sad, he suddenly cleans the whole house. He wants to make me happy and he knows I like everything clean, even if my sadness that day didn't have to do with the dirt!"

Yeah. We want to know how we get them to do that!

The 10 Best Things You Can Do Together in Total and Complete Silence

1. Read.
2. Sleep (duh . . .).
3. Have sex. (Try it. It can be wildly erotic—even turn off the heavy breathing.)
4. Eat.
5. Have a staring contest.
6. Drive. (Turn off the music and just sit together watching the hills roll by.)
7. Go for a swim. (Silence underwater can be incredibly satisfying!)
8. Have Silent Wednesdays. (Try it for an hour and see what you learn. TV off, stereo off, voices off.)
9. Watch a beautiful movie muted and don't talk to each other. Let the images say everything!
10. Go for a walk. (Sometimes just being together, holding hands, can communicate everything you need to hear.)

Opening Up

We all know the chick at the party who's known you for all of seven minutes before she's managed to communicate her entire wretched childhood and the names of all the bullies in her eighth-grade class who ever pushed her down in mud. But some of us weren't born with the "tell all" gene. Some might argue that this is a good thing. But others would say it is really important to be able to open up, especially to people with whom we share an intimate relationship. "Remember that you've already accepted him and go from there," emphasizes Lauree Ostrofsky. "The more you let him in, the stronger the relationship will be."

But it is simultaneously important that we recognize how to create an environment in which someone is emotionally prepared to confide in us.

Dianna points out that her guy's affection and ability to confide in her is something pretty special. "It's huge for this man who's very quiet, private, and closed to most everyone. I'm the one who's let inside."

So, what if your boyfriend is one of the closed ones and you are concerned that he is no longer opening up to you the way you'd like him to?

Relationship expert Christy Calame asks you to look at a few factors—for instance, "If they were brought up in a home where the modeling was negative, they might find this new level of commitment to be a negative experience." Decide for yourself if you are prepared to help him through these issues. And then work to foster a positive and nonjudgmental environment in which he can bare his soul.

> ### WHY YOU SHOULD OPEN UP TO HIM
>
> You've already accepted each other. What could go wrong?
>
> You may strengthen your relationship.
>
> It's good to have someone in whom you can confide and vice versa.

One way to do this is to take a lesson from the chatty Kathy at the party cited at the beginning of the section. If the information belongs to him, don't share it. Talking about your relationship is a natural way to communicate with our friends. But if you are trying to make him feel safe sharing his personal info with you, take it easy on the gossip. This means both to him about your other friends, as it might make him nervous that his secrets are unsafe, as well as watching what you share with your friends about his life. After a while you will find you have a man who can tell you anything. And with that comes the security that you too can share anything with him.

HOW TO ENCOURAGE HIM OPENING UP TO YOU

Don't be judgmental when he tells you things.

Keep his secrets safe.

Open up to him. It's a reciprocal process.

When we asked Marilyn, a banker in New York City, if living with her boyfriend helped her to get to know him better she answered, "It had to. He *had* to talk to me now."

Which is true. So together, do your best to make it a long and pleasant conversation!

what to expect when you move in—and beyond

Sam and I seemed to be on the same page about everything, and I thought living together would be so romantic. Then we moved in. And I realized all the ways we were on completely different pages, in completely different books, in different sections of different bookstores in distant cities on opposite ends of the world. I love to sleep in—he pops out of bed ready to have a chipper conversation, which of course annoys the crap out of me. I could just have a simple mac and cheese or a salad for dinner—late—but as soon as he gets home from work, he wants to start cooking a full dinner of pot roast with potatoes, carrots, and God knows what else. Then, I 'get in trouble' when I have to work late and dinner is cold. On a Friday night, he wants to stay out with his friends until 4 A.M. and then spend all day Saturday in front of the TV recovering. But Saturdays are the days I want to spend time doing things with him, like shopping or going for long bike rides. It's frustrating that he's not interested. Plus I'm starting to think he looks really gross sitting there on the couch in his boxers with his hand in a bag of Doritos, all puffy-eyed. So not romantic.

—Ashley, sales representative, Boston, Massachusetts

Everyone goes into a live-in relationship with different expectations. Some expect it to be a fun-filled sleepover every night. Others picture endless evenings of long, romantic candlelit dinners followed by some very naughty desserts. Some are so excited to have someone to share the rent and utility bills that they haven't really thought things completely through. Others are just plain scared.

But if there's anything Renee learned from her live-in experience, it's that, as she puts it, "nothing is perfect." We're not saying to become a Debbie Downer and just be expecting—and pointing out to yourself—the worst all the time. Quite the opposite, we want you to make the most of it. To do that, you *must* realize that it will probably be a big adjustment to live with your guy, and that you'll constantly need to be adjusting and readjusting to each other. It's like being in a bed that's just a little too small with your guy. Limbs everywhere, and nowhere to put them. But you can find enjoyment there. We mean, who can't figure out a way to make a bed that's too small fun? It's a bed! No, it probably won't be too difficult. It may just take a little extra effort and positive thinking.

"Being with someone always takes work," says Laura. Some couples find signs of trouble right off the bat. Why? "The beginning of the experience has a whole range of emotions," says Carrie. Emotions always make for more tenuous situations. Agreed?

Plus the fact that you share a home can totally change the dynamic, including what you do when you're upset. Suddenly, you might not be able to hide from a problem or keep your feelings a secret. "It was after our first loud disagreement that I realized I didn't have any place to run away," says Jeanette. "This was my house now, my old apartment was gone and I was going to have to stay and deal with whatever problem started it."

What Was the Easiest Part of Learning to Live With Him?

"Knowing that each night I would sleep next to him . . . and that he made me feel more relaxed." —Marie, Philadelphia

"House décor, as we have similar tastes." —Amanda, San Francisco

"Having someone around the apartment who can fix and take care of things I didn't know how to do myself." —Hope, Southampton

"Sharing the bathroom and bedroom on workdays. This surprised me a lot, since I get up considerably earlier. We worked out a routine pretty quickly. He stays in bed and I don't turn on a whole lot of lights." —Jeanette, Reston

"Once the house is clean and the yard work is done, you can just relax and be together." —Renee, Columbus

So, how to cope with all these changes? "Go into it with an open mind and be flexible," says Amanda. Because when you're in close quarters with someone, you're bound to piss each other off, much like siblings or roommates—but maybe even worse, because all those emotions we mentioned earlier are involved. Just remember the fact that you can't escape him may actually bring you two closer. Jeanette explains: "It didn't ruin the fun. In a way it made our commitment to each other stronger." Really, all that arguing and annoyance that comes with adjusting to living with someone can actually be *good* for your relationship.

"Anger and annoyance are facets of you," points out life coach Lauree Ostrofsky. "Strengthening any relationship is all about being able to show each other who you are. And," she goes on, "expressing what is important to you it part of that."

There are other couples who start off great but have some issues rear their ugly heads later. "I had a coworker who moved in with her boyfriend. I remember asking her a few weeks in how it was going. She got all excited and bubbly, saying, 'It's like living with your best friend!' She didn't have one bad thing to say. A year later, they were selling their condo and splitting up," says Ashley.

What could have gone wrong? Well, we don't know that couple personally, but maybe they were blindsided by rocky times later on and didn't know how to deal with them. Ostrofsky suggests always having a big picture to refer back to. "When you move in, make sure you are clear with yourself about what is important to you for your home. How do you want to *be* with this other person?"

WHAT TO EXPECT WHEN YOU MOVE IN

You may feel unexpected emotions.

You can't run away when you're upset.

You're bound to piss each other off, at least a little, at least *some*times.

You could become closer.

It could be easy in the beginning and more difficult *later*.

You'll have to be flexible to make it work.

From the start, you'll be setting precedents and goals for the future of your relationship.

You'll be required to change and grow together.

It might take some time to solve some issues. But you can do it!

Have a long-term idea about how you see yourselves, both separately and together! Accept early on that conflict will inevitably be a part of this, but as long as greater goals are being met, you can trust you remain on the right track, or a track that is close to the track you meant to be on. You know, not like a train track, or a gutter ball track in bowling. Right. The point is, look at where and who you both are in the moment and truthfully ask yourself how you hope things will evolve. The fact is, growing together sometimes can be hugely benefited by setting common goals. Unfortunately, we're not suggesting you won't have to also be a little flexible.

The longevity of a relationship relies on the two people's ability to go with the flow. In Renee's experience: "Fighting—really fighting—didn't seem to happen until later on in the living-together process. And that's always a hard thing to get through. I think that first big fight can tell you a lot about a person. And a lot about yourself. How you apply that knowledge determines how often—and how intensely—you fight in the future," says Renee.

In the beginning, when it comes to everything from argument protocol to the kind of movies you rent together, you'll be setting precedents for what's okay in the relationship going forward.

For Carrie and her boyfriend, the hot-button issue was staying out late at night with friends without checking in with each other. It was a common cause of debate that eventually they solved together. "I think after a few good fights it was just something that was understood: If you're going to be late, just call," says Carrie. "It didn't ruin the fun of living together. It actually made it more real, and gave me a better sense of responsibility and ownership."

Roller Coasters Are Supposed to Be Fun

Okay, so you made it through the beginning and are well on your way on your cohabitational journey. Maybe you're feeling a bit like Hope: "One minute I could think he is adorable and the next minute I want to scream."

She is not alone. Relationships are cyclical. There are ups and downs and plateaus and valleys. There will be times when you're drunk with love and times when you're wondering how you ended up with someone who picks his nose while he's surfing the Web.

"Just *know* that people go through these ups and downs, and don't give them more meaning than they should have," says Melissa. "A week of being extra sensitive about the dishes does *not* mean that we're doomed to break up." This takes a large dose of realism. We have to forget all those romance novels we read when we were fourteen and accept things as they come.

Don't dwell on little issues—they're not what your relationship is all about. "I think when you spend that much time with someone, and you live that closely, there will inevitably be times when you look at him or her and wonder, 'What was I thinking?'" says Renee. "Those are the times when it's so critical to remember why you fell in love in the first place." That's why injecting a little romance here and there is so important—and reminding yourself that neither of you can be perfect all the time.

"The guard is down," Ostrofsky reminds us. "Think of it as *getting* to have bad days in front of each other. Appreciate that you are allowing each other to see yourselves at all your levels."

It's a good thing, agrees Amanda. "Grow from it—and don't compare your relationship to others as each partnership is different."

That's right, you will have to come up with your own ways of dealing with conflict, annoyance and anger. For example, Jeanette and her guy sometimes hash it out with help from the computer. "We e-mail each other if we can't find the words to say something in person," says Jeanette. "I love e-mail! Sometimes it's nice to just say what you need to say and not be interrupted."

"I would say that if you love him and you want to be with him, all the so-called bad stuff is worth it. It makes him who he is—the person you fell in love with," says Marie.

So it won't be perfect. It will be an

HOW TO DEAL WITH UPS AND DOWNS
Be prepared for them and the fact that they're totally normal. Knowing is half the battle.
Maintain realistic expectations. This is not a fairy tale.
Don't dwell on the small things.
Inject romance where you can.
Learn to actually appreciate the bad stuff. It can bring you closer.
Come up with your own way of resolving bad feelings and conflict.
Remember that it's worth it because it means you're with the guy you love.
Just deal with it. Sometimes you can't explain how.

adventure. And what's wrong with a little adventure? If you get through it, it will be an amazing experience. And if you're lucky enough, it may even be easy.

"I can't even remember how we handled most of our difficult situations. We just did," says Amanda. "I am sure we had some issues, but they were never major. Sorry if this is sappy, but if you love each other, you work it out. You just live and deal with each other's oddities. No need to make mountains out of molehills."

Breaking Up: What We Don't Want to Talk About

We're here to celebrate cohabitation, so we really don't want to dwell on breakups. But with us talking about the ups and downs of living together, we must mention that some downs don't always go back up. Breakups happen. And it's not the end of the world. Hear what our real women have to say:

"The bad stuff makes you realize that the good times are really good. That is what makes a relationship. If you can't get past the bad, then it isn't much of a relationship . . . When it turns out not to be a fairy tale then you need to decide whether this is something you want for the rest of your life." —Carrie, New York City

"I really hope that anyone who is living with someone and sees an unhealthy pattern can recognize it and get out of that situation. No one deserves to be in a relationship that is always driving you crazy or is unhealthy no matter how much you love the person. If it doesn't work out you still get all that wonderful experience that cannot be replaced and it will allow you to make an even better choice in the future." —Jeanette, Reston

"You can only be so flexible, so if the living arrangement isn't working out, don't look at it as a failure or consider yourself a failure, look at it as a learning experience."—Amanda, San Francisco

"I wanted to get married after a certain point . . . Jon could have just 'lived in sin' with me forever. So, after a certain point, I had to do what was best for me. I told him at one point, when we had nine months left on our lease, that he had nine months to decide whether or not he wanted to marry me. I told him I respected where he was in his life, but I also had to be true to myself. So as painful as it would be to leave him, if he wasn't ready to make the commitment, I would. I asked that he be true to himself, too. If he wasn't ready—that was fine. I was fully ready to accept and respect that decision. Thankfully, he came to his senses and proposed four days before the 'deadline.' I mean, Christ, we had been together for over six years at that point, so I would like to think it wasn't that tough of a decision to make!"—Donna, Secaucus, New Jersey

Paula Abdul Was on to Something—Maybe

Maybe you've had one of those opposites-attract kind of romances. Or maybe it's the classic situation where you feel you have so many big things in common, and then you move in and all those little differences seem, well, gigantic. The key word here is *seem*. Remember, the fact that he hits snooze twenty times while you're still trying to get your last hour of REM sleep is a small deal—even though it may not seem so tiny at 6 A.M.

"Many things are different between us—I like dancing, he hates it," says Laura. "I like disco, he likes rock-and-roll. He likes flying airplanes, I won't even get *in* a little plane. We found the things we had in common and focused on those: religion, background, child rearing, work ethic. We put less importance on the differences, and more on the similarities. My husband agrees to dance with me at work events, and I agree that he can go flying on the weekends. It's all about give and take."

Okay, for the two-thousandth time, (say it with us) *communicate* with him. Tell him your wants and needs—then work together to find a compromise. Maybe he can set his alarm a little later, so there are less hits on the snooze button before he actually rises and shines. This will take some problem-solving skills.

"Socially we are complete opposites. . . . He can talk to anyone and I am somewhat shy and don't like to go places where I don't know anyone. He likes to go out and I love to stay home. I think since we are opposites our social calendar is very balanced with small dinners with friends and large parties. We really didn't figure this out until we moved in together because . . . then we went out more as a couple and we realized that socially our schedule was all over the place," says Carrie.

So even when it comes to the minute details of your day-to-day life, you will have to make some adjustments here and there.

"I learned that Marc needs more 'Marc time' than I do. Meaning, he needs more time to himself. So I had to learn to let him have that," says Amanda.

Just keep on looking on the bright side the way Amanda did—like her, you may even learn to appreciate the differences. Renee did, too: "I'm an early riser, and at least two of my live-ins were major sleeper-in-ers. I started off resenting that, but eventually I learned that I liked having that time to myself. I could use it to clean, to play music, to just lie in front of the TV and watch movies, to exercise, to do absolutely whatever I wanted. It became my quiet time. Now if it gets interrupted, I get a little resentful of *that*," she laughs.

Of course it isn't all about positive thinking. In this case, Ostrofsky wants us to go back to a concept she pointed out in an earlier chapter, that of "eyes on your paper." In other words, she says. "You have to figure out if a decision affects you or him.

. . . If it is a question of a morning person and a night person, that's easy . . . It isn't about you. What matters, however, is that you find quality time to be together when both of you are awake." Bottom line? Don't worry if you have your differences. Differences aren't a problem as long as you don't make them a problem. But noticing what becomes problematic in those differences and solving *that,* well, that's where things get synched up. Therein lies the harmony!

WHEN YOU'RE LIVING WITH YOUR OPPOSITE

Focus on what you have in common.

Downplay the differences.

Make compromises where you can.

Communicate—our favorite word.

Figure out what's good about being different.

Learn not to dwell.

See if there are ways you two can learn from each other.

Don't try to change each other! You love each other as you are.

Hey, and you might even learn a little bit from each other. Hope and her guy rubbed off on each other after living together for a while. She explains: "He has learned to keep things relatively neat and be more organized. I have learned to do more maintenance around the house from his teaching me. And I've learned to be more patient with projects and take my time. He's even started eating more vegetables—he ate almost none before!"

Of course, for the love of Pete, don't look at this as an opportunity to try to change each other. You are living with this guy because you love *him,* not because he's a project. "I can remember when our oldest child asked me how I 'tamed' her father, since he had been a bit on the wild side when we moved in—a biker, a drinker, you-name-it-he-did-it kinda guy," says Laura. "I told her that relationships take work, and that there is no changing anyone unless they want to participate in the change. If you are willing to move in with someone, you better be willing to negotiate change for the betterment of you both. If you care about the other, you will get through things just fine."

A General Move-in Timeline (Chronology May Vary)

Week 1: Who loves you, my wittle Shmoopy Woopy Doopy?

Week 2: You're fabulous.

Week 3: Love ya.

Week 4: Um, could you turn the TV/Wii/porn *off* once in a while?

Week 5: Did you always breathe that loudly?

Week 6: Maybe you should try a career shift. Something that involves travel. Like trucking. Yeah. You'd make a great trucker.

Week 7: What do you mean you are busy tonight? What about ME?

Week 8: What did I do before I had my baby around to move the cars on winter mornings and help me remember to get my oil changed?

Week 9: Who loves you, my wittle Shmoopy Woopy Doopy?

When the Going Gets Tough

Now you live together and, as Leigh, a writer in New York, puts it, "I can't leave if we fight. I have nowhere to go and I have to deal with it."

But that sentiment extends beyond just fighting. The fact is, now that you live together, more than before, you are saying with your actions that you are in it. Even though no one has a ring and no member of the clergy made you swear before a crowd of people you love, it does sort of mean for better or worse.

And things do sometimes get worse. Like there are those times when life hands you proverbial lemons. Or those times when life makes paper cuts all over your body and squeezes lemon juice all over them and then shoves the juiced lemon up your ass. It does. And when you live with someone, they sometimes end up with lemon juice in their eye. What with all that sour lemon flying around it'd be tough not to get some there. So how do you manage to respect your partner even when all hell is breaking loose in your own life?

"I had a back injury where I ripped three discs in my back and was in physical therapy for a couple months," says Leigh. "He was very helpful in taking care of me. He once carried me up twelve flights of stairs when the elevator was out in the building and I was having a back spasm."

It is fair to expect that your partner will go out of his way on your behalf when things are tough. After all, it shows respect and compassion, two very real indicators that you have found yourself a good man. But make sure that on your end you have respect and compassion for him. While it isn't easy to go through life's shitty days, it isn't always easy to be the guy carrying the girl up twelve flights. Try to remember that. At least a little.

But consider if the roles were reversed. Sometimes other people's depressions are downright . . . depressing! It can be really hard to take on another person's pain. Leigh also mentions a time when things went badly for her guy. "He had a severe manic episode and had to be committed to the mental institution. He was diagnosed with bipolar disorder. I visited him every day in the hospital."

GET THROUGH THE REALLY TOUGH STUFF TOGETHER
Take care of each other.
Have respect and compassion for each other, no matter who is going through the tougher time.
Just being there for each other can be the best medicine.
Remember that you're a team now.
If you want to make it for the long haul, than stick through it for the long haul.

Generally speaking, the rules of compassion, while far from finite, are fairly simple. Maggie says, "Just being there for one another was the best support . . . no matter day or middle of the night."

Look, you are a team now, even if you are not a legal team. You likely have matching team uniforms (we hope not literally) and you might sometimes be called upon to pitch (again, not literally, at least if you are inside with a lot of expensive glass around). Try to remember that this can bring about some of the best things about people: we get the opportunity to support each other through the tough stuff! If you view it as a liability or a pain in the ass, you are missing out on some potentially wonderful intimacy.

When things have gone badly for Kerry, regardless of the situation, she says, "He basically kept a calm head and eventually calmed me down and supported me. Even when I did something wrong. I would end up being more upset than he was. And he never gave up on me."

What isn't special about that?

the benefits of cohabitation

I do know of several couples who wanted to live together, and whose parents objected so they got married, and in not too long a time ended up divorced. But so what? I also know couples who lived together first and still got divorced. And I know couples on both sides of living together before marriage, whose marriages are just fine—five, fourteen, and twenty-one years later. I'm sure there is data out there that could pull the argument one way or another, but every one of us is an exception to the numeric rules, so I say ignore them. AND, I also say, cohabitation doesn't improve marriage or increase the likelihood of its demise. Living with a boyfriend or skipping straight to marriage are both right for some people, and wrong for some people, for completely individual reasons.

—Karen

We hope that as you've read this book you have come to realize that, while we want you to take away some of the awesome advice from these women who have lived with their boyfriends, everyone's experience is different. Our last bit of advice is pretty simple: advice is just that, and should never be a substitute for doing what is best for you.

Wait! Don't stomp your foot and ask the heavens why you wasted precious hours memorizing the wisdom of that one lady who proposed a time-out over chucking some broccoli at her man's head! A book like this was meant to dispel myths, to point out things you may never have thought of, and to make you realize reasons why you have no problem saying certain things to your man in ways you would never think to disrespect a co-worker or buddy.

> **WHAT TO TAKE AWAY FROM THIS BOOK**
>
> Do what's best for you!
>
> Adapt the advice of the real women to suit your individual relationship.
>
> Re-examine your relationship with respect to the topics we've covered.
>
> Consider changes you might make to some of your negative behaviors or thoughts.
>
> Be inspired to some new ideas for improving some aspect of your live-in situation.

But most importantly, by reading it, you were given a minute to put away impulsivity, to temper impatience, to take some time to consider how to proceed deliberately and with the best possible results for the two of you.

Having said that, let's say you moved in, your communication was impeccable, your design scheme flawless. All went swimmingly, smashingly (how could it not, you smart lady? You read the book!) and suddenly you are wondering quite simply . . . now what?

You see, dear girl, in this book we answer that, too.

I Do . . . Don't I?

There you are, at your favorite basketball team's game. You can see yourself on the JumboTron with an illustrated heart juxtaposed around your head and you look back at your guy—your live-in

MOVING-IN MANTRA: ON ADVICE

"Advice is what we ask for when we already know the answer but wish we didn't."—ERICA JONG

love—he's on one knee. Or maybe it's a romantic dinner and a chocolate dessert is capped with a diamond instead of a cherry. Perhaps it is at the grocery store after he snuck off to spend ten dollars in quarters trying to win the plastic ring in one of those quarter machines so he could propose in the produce aisle, since that was where you met.

"Does cohabitation *have* to lead to marriage?" you ask yourself. "Shouldn't I be more ready for this?" you wonder. After all, you've seen his Spidey pajamas and that didn't scare you off.

Maura, a film producer in New York, explains that she and her guy aren't getting married because they have other priorities. "Both of us are busy with careers and other things right now. *We* both recognize the importance and seriousness of our relationship, why should we care if the government does?"

So, the answer is, plainly, that cohabitation does not inevitably lead to marriage. As we've mentioned, it's an opportunity for you two to grow into a cohesive unit that does or does not require legal attention. Or it might mean growing apart. Both have merit. Both sentences, as you've noticed, use the word "grow," and that means neither is a bad thing.

Marriage, like cohabitation, is a symbolic way to further a relationship. For some people, it has an even deeper meaning. At weddings you might hear brides and grooms acknowledging that they have chosen the father or mother of their children. Hopefully,

DOES COHABITATION HAVE TO LEAD TO MARRIAGE?

Remember that marriage is simply a spiritual and/or legal recognition of your union.

You could grow together during cohabitation—or grow apart.

Living together will help you decide whether or not you want to marry him.

Living together may change *you*, too.

your having lived together will have helped you to make an informed decision about whether or not this is the best man for the job of co-piloting your life and having a massive imprint on the lives of your children (if you're planning on having them).

Or let's just say you went from being single to suddenly having to navigate the pitfalls of a relationship and cohabitation at the same time. How did it change? How did you successfully go from a girl at the single's mixer to a girl in the spoon position? And how can things become even better than they ever were?

Two Minus One

How does life change, not just from footloose-and-fancy-free couple to cohabiting couple, but also from being single to half of a live-in arrangement? Maybe in your case, you just wake up and feel like you are suddenly beholden to someone else, or maybe it is something more literal. Heidi explains, "I moved in and within two weeks I was dating the guy who lived in the bedroom above mine. It was a three-bedroom house that had a couple living in bedroom number three. It didn't take long before I went from totally single to living with a boyfriend."

When you were single you never had to let anyone know where you were or what you were doing. You could make deci-

sions for yourself—pack up and move to Uzbekistan, go dancing, FLIRT! Judith felt like the biggest change for her was "Never
being able to just go when I wanted to go without that phone call.
I always thought I had to ask permis-
sion." Courtney misses "being able to
navigate the remote control."

"Sometimes I just want to wander around and not have to have an
expected ETA home," says Kerry. "As
a couple living together, it's kind of
expected that you know where the
other one is at all times."

It is possible to weave those sweet
joys of singledom into a successful relationship. The difference is that you do
have someone else to consider. Even
Kerry admits, "It's not that he makes
me tell him where I am at all times!" It

WHAT CHANGES AS A RESULT OF COHABITATION?
You might feel more a part of a "couple."
You might feel less free when it comes to making major life changes.
You might not feel okay with flirting with other guys.
You might need to be more accountable for your where-abouts at all times.
You might want to divulge all the details of your day to him.
You might not miss being single at all!

is still respecting your boyfriend to say you have a few things to do
and not get into it until later when you are snuggled down for the
night. Then you can tell him all about the spontaneous walk you
took around downtown and the amazing gargoyles on one of the
buildings you'll have to show him someday!

It's kind of a fair trade. You now have a live-in partner in
crime, gin rummy opponent, and road trip buddy. And we might
even go so far as to advise holding on to some of those singleton
perks. No one ever said a girl couldn't flirt. Julie suggests, "Now
that I live with my boyfriend, if I am talking to men in the world,
it is suddenly free of subtext. It is *me* talking to *them,* not a single

girl talking to a guy who may or may not be single—which is just so much more fun than worrying about what my body language is saying—or what theirs is telling me." In other words, it takes the complications out of flirting because ain't no one gettin' any later. Isn't that liberating?

And how about this totally revolutionary idea: flirt with your boyfriend! We don't just mean doing one of your patented closed mouth burp with a harmonizing fart. We're talking batting those lashes. Putting your hand on his arm and throwing your head back to laugh when he says something funny. We want you to do it with your tits, ass, and sweet sweet smile.

So what if you lose some of the fun of collecting phone numbers and first kisses. Now you have a sure thing to go home with at the end of the night! So maybe the bit of respect and responsibility you now have to show each other can be a totally bearable side effect to an otherwise happy cohabitation.

In fact, says Maggie, "Other than freedom from being responsible to another person, I don't miss anything about being single."

What's New, Pussycat?

Okay, let's say he is your number one, the guy you need to share your victories and miseries with, the face you most like to see when you wake up in the morning, or while you're having an orgasm. Right. This is the guy? Good. How will it all (or won't it all) change?

"Yes, we ended up married, and there was not much difference afterward," acknowledges Laura. "We discussed this possibility prior to us even moving in together. We did that just to ensure we could live and grow together."

You have to expect that your experience of having already merged much of your lives through cohabitation is going to limit how different being married feels. The fact is, one outdated idea claims that the first year of marriage is the hardest. But having already ironed out issues of space and personal commitment is one way that this transition might actually prove far smoother than it would be for a couple that marries before living together.

That doesn't mean *nothing* changes. You are deepening your commitment, altering your relationship. If cohabiting means you are allowed to keep one foot out the door, marriage might seem like that door just slammed shut with both of you inside.

> **IF WE GET MARRIED, HOW WILL OUR RELATIONSHIP CHANGE?**
>
> There might be a strengthening of a spiritual or emotional bond between you two.
>
> It might feel more serious and more permanent.
>
> You might become closer to his family—and actually feel like you *are* his family.
>
> It might not change much at all.

Jen, an after-school coordinator in Brooklyn, New York noticed that even though she and Todd lived together before marriage, "For that first year we were married, I'd have these moments where I'd hear him breathing loudly and I'd feel completely panicked so I'd go, 'are you going to do that forever?'"

Amanda had a different experience after she and Marc got married. "Not much was physically different, but spiritually, I did feel the bond was different. Much stronger and sweeter. Not much changed other than emotions."

For Lucy, it was the little things that changed after she and Ryan tied the knot. "I could actually order a pizza and give the last name 'Sullivan' honestly." Remember that the changes could go further than just what's between you and him. "It seems things naturally changed as far as becoming closer with his family and spending more time with them," says Lucy.

Renee puts it this way: "I married two of my live-in boyfriends. In the first case, I was hoping things would change and they didn't. In the second, I was hoping they wouldn't . . . and they didn't."

In other words, we don't know what's going to happen. But at least you have the info gathered throughout your cohabitation that will help you both make a good decision.

"I feel as though marriage is forever and that's a long, long, long time," explains Jeanette. "Living together is wonderful practice and the most valuable thing you can possibly do for yourself and your relationship. If it doesn't work out you still get all that wonderful experience that cannot be replaced and it will allow you to make an even better choice in the future."

Ultimately, what lessons have been learned by women who have lived with their guys? What should you know before you take the plunge? What should you remind yourself as you sit there in your living room listening to him sing off-key in the shower?

Maura says, "It's not perfect, relationships are not perfect. To anyone who thinks moving in or marrying someone is going to solve problems, please take a reality pill before doing so."

etymology lesson

The slang verb "to shack up" first appeared with the meaning "to cohabit," in 1935 by the author, Zora Neale Hurston. The expression "living in sin" to mean "cohabit without marriage" first appeared in 1938.

Laura moved in with a man who later became her husband of twenty-one years. "Neither of us wanted to relive the mistakes of our first marriages so we wanted to 'check each other out' prior to making the ultimate commitment."

Do as I Say

"If we had waited until we were married to share space, I would have felt trapped and overwhelmed by all the 'huge' changes in my life all at once," recalls Chris. "This made committing to the relationship more like easing into a cold swimming pool—one step at a time! And we did learn that we'd be a pretty great married couple."

For Lucy it was about learning what was important and growing together. "I watched him blossom from a student getting his master's degree in Slavic Linguistics to a self-taught computer technologist to a successful project manager in IT . . . Sometimes I feel we have been married longer because we have lived together before and known each other for almost half of our adult life!"

"My expectation was to figure out if the feelings I had toward Stefan would last through the mundane life tasks," says Jeanette. "And to see if I was going to be able to live with him for the rest of my life."

"I knew I was head-over-heels in love with him, but I was still asking myself: 'Is this feeling for forever?'" says Rita, a chef in Jersey City, New Jersey.

Big questions, people. Ask yourself the big questions.

But what if you live together and the lessons you learn sadly lead you to conclude that your relationship is not ready to deepen

WHAT LESSONS HAVE REAL WOMEN LEARNED ABOUT COHABITATION?
Relationships aren't perfect.
Cohabitation allows you to check each other out before marriage.
It's like easing into a cold swimming pool—allows you to take your time getting to the next level.
You'll grow, change—and maybe mature—together.
It will let you ask yourself the big questions about your relationship to help you figure out where you're going.
You might figure out that it's not the right relationship for you.

or, worse, should probably be abandoned before you both start going down with the ship?

Katie, an industrial designer in Los Angeles, California says, "The relationship suffered because I didn't want to make compromises with my dreams, which translated down to both day-to-day and long-term decisions. This made it an unbalanced and an unstable environment for both of us . . . I am grateful for my experience, however, because I can move on to other relationships with this lesson learned and offer more of myself with confidence that I have the ability to be a part of a lasting relationship."

And Becky, an account executive in Cleveland, points out that if you do realize you have to get out, "A woman can learn so much about herself and her ability to 'take on the world' just by having her own apartment, paying bills, changing light bulbs, etc."

You never know. The "et cetera" that Becky mentions of living on your own might be the biggest growth of all!

Superlatives

Finally, it is time to acknowledge the best and worst things about living together. For Becky the best is "being together." The worst is

"Scott leaving his empty beer/water/pop cans all over the house." "Best: sex and companionship," says Renee. "Worst: no alone time." Hope claims that for her, "the overall worst—you lose that fun, giddy Friday-afternoon feeling when you would see each other after five days being apart. The overall best feeling—you lose that lousy Sunday night feeling going home and knowing you will not be together again for five days!!"

For Amanda the downside was minimal compared to this great positive. "Finally making a nest and calling it home," she says. "After years of having roommates and just having a house, I was finally making myself a home. With roommates, I never wanted to invest in nice things—'cause what if they ruined them? I loved buying furniture, etc. with Marc and feeling as if we were really starting to build our life together. I guess there is something symbolic in buying a coffee table together!"

Lucy says, "The best thing about living with a boyfriend was obviously being able to see that person whenever you wanted—all of the time. Of course you could save on renting two places! The worst thing might have been missing out on some of the maturing I would have done living independently. I also wonder if my relationships with my girlfriends would have been stronger or different if I hadn't lived with my boyfriend."

Chris discovered there was one thing she really liked: "Finding out how much better and easier it was than I thought it'd be." Of course she could have lived without cleaning up after someone else. "That was the worst," she says.

For Maura, the support system living with her guy gives her is tops. But she does admit, "I can't keep ice cream or sweets in the house because he eats them all before I get a chance to."

Boiling It Down

You're a woman who's deciding whether or not to live with a guy. Or you're a woman trying to see if she can improve her live-in situation. Or perhaps you're a woman who's cohabiting and is considering her next step.

We hope that you have been armed with some tools, and been fed bits and pieces to chew on. This is a big decision you are making—or have made. But so is having sex for the first time, or choosing who will give you your first big smooch. We want you to think about cohabitation as a big step, but maybe slightly less big a step than it was once considered in our society. We want you to see why it is both easier and harder than you thought it would be. We want to both clear up the old notions and stick a few spokes in some of the new ones.

Did we sufficiently confuse you? Then our work is done.

Just kidding!

It is our intention to slow you down, give you the chance to scan the horizon, peruse your options, validate your decisions, and overall become smarter, savvier, and better able to handle whatever choices you make.

As Katie notes, "More women of our generation have the ability to choose a family or a career as a way of life or anything in between. We have more examples of successful women to follow, more encouragement to dream about our potential, and more opportunity to educate ourselves to make these things happen under our own accord."

So we live at a time when we are able to make the choice to live with the man we love. Erika, for one, can't think of a downside to that. "The best thing was definitely being closer to him! I loved having him around, coming home at the end of the day and knowing we'd be together."

And isn't that the whole idea?

index

about the authors

ELENA DONOVAN MAUER is a writer and editor specializing in relationships and women's service. Her writing has appeared in publications such as *Psychology Today*, *Modern Bride*, *Lifetime* magazine, and *Bridal Guide*. She and her live-in guy have been married since 2003. She lives in New York City.

JOSELIN LINDER is a writer and filmmaker. She is the author of *The Purity Test*, a book of questions based on the online phenomenon. She is also a founding member of the Stoned Crow Writers Workshop, a fiction group that has carried on a weekly meeting since 2005. She currently lives and works in Brooklyn, New York. Her boyfriend just moved in . . . and they got a dog. Gulp.